Animals
1—

Living with the Animals

Living with the Animals

EDITED BY

Gary Indiana

Faber and Faber
BOSTON · LONDON

First published in the United States in 1994 by Faber and Faber, Inc., 50 Cross Street, Winchester, MA 01890.

This paperback edition first published in 1995.

Library of Congress Cataloguing-in-Publication Data

Living with the animals / edited by Gary Indiana.
    p.   cm.
   ISBN 0-571-19875-9 (paper)
    1. Human-animal relationships.   2. Animals.   3. Pets
  I. Indiana, Gary.
  QL85.L58   1994
  155.9'1—dc20   94-19207
                                       CIP

Cover design by Mary Maurer
Cover photograph by John Sann

Contents

v

Introduction

BRIEFLY, THEN: the idea of this book suggested itself when one writer at a party somewhat rudely told another writer, "You're going to do your best work when you finally figure out what you're interested in." The second writer indignantly reported the remark to a third writer, who, in those dark days before Prozac, himself became rattled by it, confessing that he was no longer interested in anything. "Well, what do you care about?" A long, thoughtful pause.

"My cat."

By the time this chain letter of anxiety reached me, I had already noted that many writers and artists of my acquaintance were just nuts about animals, and that few had actually mirrored this infatuation in their work. Some, of course, had, quite spectacularly. But it seemed to me that most of us, writing our books, making our movies, painting our paintings, have an awkward relationship to other species, and nature in general. Something unresolved, fragmented, marginalized, fractured; a pentimento of genetic memory; less grandly, a guilty knowledge that other forms of life are disappearing to make room for more of us.

As other people have observed, one's sphere of moral action in the modern world is usually completely inadequate to a given predicament, which leads to frustration and irrational behavior. We can't really save the planet by writing a check to a conservation fund, though maybe it helps a little; the Discovery channel, wonderful as it is, can be a cosmic bummer, reminding us at every turn that all the world's creatures are on a collision course with economic development, civil wars, and other human effluvia.

The impulse to frame a lament for our vanishing companions was one I ended up resisting. For literary purposes, at least, better to celebrate the complexity of nature's absorption into culture. If this book has any didactic purpose, it's a small one: to throw some light on how contemporary people relate to the animal world. It's meant to have the variety of a rambling Victorian zoo. The size and shape of each piece was left up to the contributors, so we have memoirs and fables, anecdotes and essays, short stories and prose poems. As editor, my main concern was to canvas a range of sensibilities and talents, and to find people whose thinking about animals went well beyond predictable sentiment. There have been many fine recent books about dogs, cats, gorillas, and dolphins, but in this book the peoples are just as interesting as the animals.

New York City
June 1994

WILLIAM S. BURROUGHS

Octopus

Now, of course, my love for the octopus is strictly platonic.
But an eighty-pound octopus flashing colors like a rainbow
. . . Ooh, la la!

You LIKE ANIMALS better than people?" he adds
with a leer of idiot cunning. "Safer, aren't they?"
"Very much more dangerous. Not being
equipped with words to hide their feelings from themselves
they are far more susceptible to fear, attachment, heartbreak.
So one assumes heavier responsibility."

When did my love for the octopus arise? In a long forgotten South Sea travel book. The bestial natives have cornered
an octopus hiding in an undersea cave. They get spears and
dance around jabbing it until it comes out moaning and
begging for mercy. That's when there arose in my being a ha-
tred for Homo Sap . . . clubbing seals, exterminating the
Tasmanian marsupial wolf.

Beasts worse than the beasts you despise.

The destiny of life on this planet has gone awry. It began
with a genetic pool containing the potential for many spe-

cies, all subject to the vague and random rules of evolution, all of equal value: a synthesis. Then comes idiot Man, setting himself up as the end product of evolution with a God-given right to exterminate, torture in senseless experiments and EAT EAT EAT, the principal occupation of Homo Sap.

Many species have been driven underground by this brutal regime. . . .

The octopus is more intelligent than any animal except the chimpanzee. Just by *watching* another octopus go through those trick-and-reward bits the observing octopus can duplicate the routine. They can learn from observation alone, without training.

The octopus is highly emotional, turning red with lust or anger and pale green with fear. What a compliment to see an octopus turn a pleased pink at sight of me.

Cousteau says they are "pathetically frightened of people." No wonder.

And, like writers, they can escape in a cloud of ink.

The octopus is subject to hysterical fear. If they are captured and put in an open tank they will bite off their tentacles in terror. I recall this account: An octopus placed in a large tank jetted frantically from one side to another until someone thought to lower an empty fifty-gallon drum to the bottom. Immediately the octopus jetted into the drum and drew in its tentacles.

I love the way an octopus undulates over obstacles instead of dodging.

Above all I love his huge eyes. His watching eyes.

I think this is one of the reasons the octopus is hated and feared:

"WHAT ARE YOU LOOKING AT?"

"Don't looka me!"

Actually the octopus does not regard humans as prey and would not be able to hold a man down or eat him with its fearsome beak. But such evil proclivities of the octopus are believed with evangelical fervor because humankind has placed them in the fear-hate niche, a niche to which the worse strains of Homo Sap will be inexorably drawn.

My dear, I love the octopus, the kind of love that has nothing to do with sex but with holding and nurturing and bringing into life a new creature, a mutant. You don't need to arrive at some field theory of love to understand how it manifests itself. Look at the way the octopus changes *color*: a flush of salmon pink washing into deep aching purple, nacreous pearl shading into a wash of underwater greens, a wave of clear electric blue.

All its *feelings* right out there right now, all indecent. No wonder it has a fear of Homo Sap, galvanized into hysterical violence by anything different from its hideous self. "It don't look to me like anything created in God's image. So it's gotta be EVIL."

Homo Sap got a short attention span. Can't even hate the same thing indefinitely. Dope fiends are OUT. Child molesters are definitely IN. . . . Seems the U.S. is honeycombed with child molestation. Same stats show a good percent of human citizens been offered indecent liberties one time or another and the children themselves are all too often the seducers.

What's the big deal here? I recall a little blond boy in Tangier. When I tried to shove him out of my room he grabbed for my crotch. Later, in Italy, his father was imprisoned for incest.

Click.
DOPE FIENDS OUT.
Click.
CHILD MOLESTERS IN.

Other creatures I have loved. A coiled green snake not more than a foot long opened its tiny jaws. I carried it carefully to the creek and released it away from the cats. What an endearing creature. Few things are more beautiful and perfect than a little green snake.

A terrible picture in the *Smithsonian* or *National Geographic*: a half-grown seal with its tail bitten off by a shark, screaming for aid from two scientists. I longed to administer morphine and antibiotics in appropriate dosages, to nurture the creature back to health.

I once had a pet crow with clipped wings. Every time it was outside and saw another crow, it cawed frantically, hopping across the lawn trying to fly. I let its wings grow and released it.

If Homo Sap has any mission, it is to enter into symbiotic relationships with other creatures on the planet—including, of course, biologic mutants and hybrids: wise old tortoises with the brain of an Einstein, exquisite lemur people, seal people, octopus tribes living in coral cities, crow and eagle men riding the wind.

The old taboos against hybrids are breaking down. A jungle rat and an octopus, coyly holding hands.

The jungle rat: "Ours is a Love that dare not squeak its name."

But Homo Sap, the end product of creation, having a Divine Right over the so-called lower animals, kills and eats them. Or exterminates by destruction of habitat. Living forever in this frozen image of superiority, humans grow more bestial by the day.

It has been said that Man "binds" time by making written records of events and passing them along, thus gaining great advantage over other animals. Fifty percent of the American population does not know we fought and lost a war in Vietnam. What are they using? Another fifty percent, according to a recent poll, said yes when asked if two people engaged in homosexual sex could become infected with AIDS even if neither was infected with the HIV virus. The Immaculate Conception again waves the antiseptic Kotex, and I ask: if no one is able to read these records, where is this wondrous time binder?

The wolverine is another animal that has been demonized. Why, they disrupt trappers' lines, get into their cabins and rip open food containers, spray their scent all about. Trappers refer to the wolverines as "the little fiends," the same trappers who inflict horrible pain on raccoons, ermine, muskrat, and countless other animals. In my book, it's the trappers who are the fiends.

If taken as pups, wolverines can easily be tamed. I've read accounts of them living with families, romping in the snow with children, never biting, never scratching, completely tame. Other members of the wolverine family make affectionate pets—mongoose, meerkat, ferret, raccoon, and playful otter.

Australia seems to have been guided into a special evolutionary track, giving rise to such anomalies as the funnel web spider, the only reliably lethal spider in the world. Unless the recently developed antivenin is at hand, the funnel web will kill young or old, man or beast. A curious reversal here, too: the male is *six times more toxic than the female*, while in the black widow the female is the deadly one.

Another Australian animal that seems to represent an evolutionary tangent is the duckbill platypus. *Roll of drums:* This mammal lays eggs! And when submerged, scooping up mouthfuls of small crustaceans and worms from the muck at the bottom, it closes its eyes and ears and appears to be guided by some form of electromagnetic radar. Strangest of all, the male platypus is equipped with a venomous spur on the instep of both legs. The sting itself, while seldom fatal, causes intense agony, comparable to that caused by a stone fish—the victim screams and tries to bash his head against any hard surface. Bitten limbs can remain disabled for months, even years. Research is underway to discover medical uses for this potent substance. Perhaps in smaller doses the venom could galvanize an arrested heart to life.

And Australia can boast the only octopus that ever poses a deadly threat to Homo Sap: the Blue Ring octopus, a tiny creature six inches or so across, found in tidal pools along the coast. Normally this octopus is a neutral gray-brown, but when it is disturbed, the rings on its body and tentacles light up and glow a clear, pulsing blue.

Two young sailors on a Sydney beach . . . they fish one from a tidal pool and amuse themselves tossing it back and forth like a Frisbee.

"Oh, look, it's turned all blue!"

The octopus slithers up one sailor's arm and nips him on the back of the neck.

"Ohhhh, I don't feel so good."

DOA ninety minutes later. Emergency room, Sydney General.

The Blue Ring's venom, tetrodotoxin is also found in the liver of the fugu fish, regarded as a delicacy in Japan. Only licensed and trained chefs are allowed to prepare it. No margin for error. Two milligrams in the bloodstream can cause death in one minute. This is the drug used in Haiti to create serviceable zombies.

How can one learn to empathize with animals? Look at the octopus. Look into his great inhuman eyes. These are not fish-cold eyes but eyes charged with emotional extremes. Flushing colors and nuances of color: aching purple, caustic reds and sepias, pale tremulous greens and yellows, clouds of deep furry black. Imagine that one's eyes are anchored in one's viscera with no intervening bones, just a flexible cartilage. Eyes that hear and feel and smell and, as Cousteau said, are pathetically frightened of Homo Sap.

At Los Alamos Ranch School—where they later made the atom bomb—A. J. Connell, the school's director, called it "the school of the future."

Boys sitting on the rocks eating, telling stories by the campfire. A badger suddenly appears. The counselor, a Southerner with the look of a politician, blasted it with a .45 automatic. I can still see the stricken animal, the sad face, bleeding, dying, rolling down the slope to a stream.

As Brion Gysin says: "Man is a bad animal!" It is still very painful for me to write it out, to re-experience it, even from a numbed perception—the horribly maimed existence that passes for healthy American boyness.

I have noted that as I become more attracted to animals, I grow more disgusted with Homo Sap and his primitive species snobbery. Of course he is the final product of evolution. All those millions and trillions of years to produce THIS?

Lizbeth

LIZBETH IS GOING on nine now, and she is slowing down a bit. Yet she makes it as plain as ever that it is a very boring thing to be a writer's dog. At any rate, I got the impression that she thought so even before we hit the road, when we still lived in the little shack on Avenue B. Then she would sit up late into the night, her paws hanging off the sofa and her head between her paws, and every time I looked up from my typewriter she would still be awake and watching me, and sometimes she would sigh.

A dog sigh is a piteous thing, for I do not suppose they do it for effect. A dog sigh must be a sincere sigh.

Now we are cramped in this little apartment and there is no comfortable place where she can sit to watch me while I fiddle with the Dumpster System 2000, or play with it, or use its modem to call electronic bulletin boards, or sometimes work with it. But she will sit up for a while anyway, on the other comfortable chair, even though she cannot watch me because the chair is on the other side of my desk. Eventually she will wander to the bedroom to sleep with Clint or to sleep on our pallet once Clint rolls her out of the bed.

She also has a place we call the Dog Cave that is just a few throw pillows on the floor under the end table. I had heard somewhere that a dog ought to have a place all its own, which does not have to be surrendered to whoever else might want it—a place, in others words, where the dog has a perfect right to be. A lot of pet theories do not work out as they are supposed to, but Lizbeth seems to have got the idea of the Dog Cave, and she does make some use of it.

As an adult I had never wanted a pet. In fact I had rather distinctly wanted not to have a pet. In my materialist frame of mind I was disgusted by the pookum-ookums-snuggum-uggums sort of affection that I imagined granny ladies lavished on their cats and their little dogs, and acid-etched in my mind was a spit-out mocking line from an early Janis Ian album: "You get your love from dogs and cats." Or something like that. I don't believe the point of the protest was really to disparage pet ownership, but the line stuck with me. If the idea of having a pet had ever occurred to me I would have thought it impractical in view of my lodgings, though I suppose in any of the cheap apartments and old houses I might have kept a cat of the outdoor sort.

(I guess it is not so boring a thing for a cat to be a writer's cat. There is the problem of someone always wanting the dictionary or the notes or the manuscript a writer's cat is sleeping on, but that is another matter.)

Jerry wanted a dog. The theory was it would be his dog, and as we were in the shack on Avenue B I could hardly object that the place was unsuitable. Lizbeth was not our first attempt at having a dog. Jerry had got a little yellow puppy in the spring. He had insisted I name it—the object being, I am sure, to make me more attached to it. I had named it Calli, for a Muse. We had it only a short time before it escaped or was stolen. Afterward we inspected the fence around the backyard more closely and discovered many small breaches.

The experience of losing Calli left me with even less enthusiasm for the idea of having a dog. But Jerry devoted many hot summer days to digging post holes, mixing Sakrete, and putting up hogwire. I knew there would be another puppy.

In August I was working the nightshift at the state lunatic asylum. I never got enough sleep. If I came directly home from work I might get five hours sleep in front of the fan before I was awakened by the heat. In the afternoon I would rest on the bed, mostly in that state of in-between, neither asleep nor fully awake. On one such afternoon something tickled my face and I brushed it away without opening my eyes. The screens were as inadequate as Calli's fence had been, and in the afternoon we had flies. But whatever it was persisted and at last I opened my eyes.

It was a puppy. It was about to become Lizbeth.

But then it was Oreo. She was black on her back and sides, except for a handsome blaze on her crest. Her underside was white, with little faded black spots. Although the reason for her litter name was obvious, both Jerry and I thought it was slightly gauche, and so he named her Lizbeth—a name I would not have chosen because my mother's name is Elizabeth.

She was six months old. Jerry had got her because the owners had determined she would be a bigger dog than they wanted. Indeed, her paws seemed enormous. She never grew quite to fulfill the promise of those paws, but this may be a trick of perspective for when I first saw her she was mostly pink puppy tummy, long legs like stilts, and paws. She was

perfectly housebroken by the time we got her, and this made
it all the easier for me to like her. Jerry told me endlessly how
much Lizbeth loved me. I assumed this was meant to manipulate me into loving her, but even as I discounted Jerry's
remarks, it seemed clear that Lizbeth favored me.

Given the condition of the shack and its furnishings, I
agreed it was pointless to insist on Lizbeth's being an outside
dog. At first I tried to hold the line at no-dogs-on-the-bed.
But she would hop onto the bed once I was asleep. My next
line was: no dogs under the covers. In the summer, of course,
I slept on the spread. When I woke around noon I would
often leave her fast asleep on the bed—for nothing gets quite
so tired nor sleeps so soundly as a puppy. After I had done
this a number of times, she began to sleep with her head on
my ankles. I suspect this was to assure she would not be left
abed alone while I was up and doing interesting things.

And everything I did seemed to interest her. Curiosity is
an attribute most often ascribed to cats, but when she was a
puppy Lizbeth's curiosity seemed insatiable. One whole afternoon she sat in the backyard watching a neighbor con-
struct rabbit hutches—which I would have understood except that the rabbits had not yet arrived. "When you don't
know nothing, everything is a learning experience," Jerry
said.

By the time the first cold front of fall moved through I
had rotated to swing shift. I made Lizbeth a dog bed of old
clothes next to the people bed, and I topped it with an un-
laundered shirt I had worn so it would be olfactorally correct. But as the sunlight did in the summer, the autumnal
winds came through the walls of the old shack. I put my

hand on Lizbeth as she lay on the dog bed. She shivered. And that was the end of no-dogs-under-the-covers.

I got a book with the thought that I would train her. I didn't. For a week or so, and at intervals afterward, I'd walk with her to the schoolgrounds in the next block, and I'd go over and over "heel" and "halt." The first time we went, I put the choke collar on her, as the book recommended, but I was rather quickly convinced that she would choke herself unconscious before she would stop pulling on the leash. I don't suppose even if I'd continued to use the choke collar I would have succeeded in training her, for I am irregular in my habits, and the day-in-day-out, slowly progressing projects are the ones that I will never master. Perhaps it is sour grapes, but once I had Lizbeth and began to notice other dogs with their masters, I always cast a jaundiced eye on dogs that seemed to me to be too well regulated. I don't think it is cruelty to train an animal well—and certainly there have been times I wished Lizbeth knew this or that command—but I do think there is a spontaneity in Lizbeth that I value and that I do not see in the furry automatons.

Jerry had an all-purpose command, "settle," which Lizbeth seemed to learn at one time, but has since forgotten. Now she knows "sit," "stop," and "come." If she is not distracted, she cannot help but sit when so commanded, yet she seems to be surprised at herself for doing it. A snap of the fingers serves to dislodge her from a chair or the bed. In the meanwhile I have managed to acquire a like amount of dog language. A raised forepaw means "let's play," or in the context of a walk, "hold up a minute." Exposing the belly is an old wolf sign of submission, although Lizbeth has more occasion to use it to mean "you may rub my belly."

The ritual of the first pellet I do not understand. She always brings the first pellet of her dry food to crunch at my feet before she will eat the rest of her food. I cannot fathom this, for it does not seem to be the same thing as when a cat will bring in the corpse of a freshly killed mouse, lizard, or sparrow. One authority has told me this is her expression of gratitude, but while I do not disbelieve that she may have something in her like gratitude, I cannot accept that she could invent this way of expressing it.

"She's the doggiest dog I ever saw," Jerry would say. And so it seems to me. This helps prevent me from anthropomorphizing her, or at least prevents my anthropomorphizing her more. I can't help feeling that sometimes, sometimes there is a thought in her head, though it be a particularly doggy thought.

The summer after she came to us, Jerry left and she stayed. I kept her out of sentiment as much as anything, but I still had work at the asylum and I was glad to have a dog at the house while I was at work. She was nearly three when we became homeless. Again I kept her out of sentiment. But when I decided to take her with me I did not think I was becoming homeless. I thought it would be troublesome hitch-hiking to Los Angeles with her, but I thought I would find a situation soon. By the time I knew we were homeless and likely to be so for a long time, or forever, I had come to see Lizbeth's value. I suppose she did something, if it was no more than to smell like a dog, to keep away raccoons and possums and rats and such when we slept in places they might have frequented. But the idea of critters in the dark never bothered me much. It was, of course, in urban places that I was happy to have her to wake me when people approached us at night. This happened often enough to convince me that I wanted never to be both homeless and dogless.

Now it seems to me that affection for a *pet* is really a fairly second-rate emotion by comparison to appreciation for an animal that may be a pet, but also serves a purpose. I had always thought that dogs were domesticated and bred away from wolves, but I have since been informed that the line of wolves and the line of dogs diverged before domestication. However that may be, I now suspect, as I did not before, that dogs were not domesticated to be lap warmers.

In some things Lizbeth seems rather dull. Fetch never much appealed to her, and always turned into keep-away. It is perfectly sensible, of course, once she has found something not to return it to someone who will merely throw it away again. Yet other dogs somehow overcome this objection. She has her flashes of brilliance. Once when she wanted a walk, she brought me her leash. Once she pointed in perfect form at a bird in a bush. Once when she was thirsty, she brought me her water bowl. Once when I had dropped some money, she found it. Once she licked me awake at an unusual hour, about half a minute before we experienced an earthquake. And once she found a five-dollar bill that I had not seen on the sidewalk. The trouble is that the "onces" were all just once—although I must admit that we have not been in enough earthquakes to make that a fair test.

It is said that animals are good judges of character, but Lizbeth seems to have no such talent. She is happy to be introduced to anyone, and will act as if anyone to whom she has been introduced is her buddy forever. What is true, and I would have done better to learn it sooner, is that some de-fects of the character of the master can be deduced from the behavior of the dog. I suppose even a bad man can be good to his dog, but a man that is mean to his dog is bound to be mean in other ways as well.

In spite of her shortcomings, as a watchdog Lizbeth has failed only once. She did sleep as we were approached by a mounted police officer when she was under the covers where we were bedded down in a park. Even then I was awake, so I was not surprised. Otherwise, if there was something to detect, she detected it, and when she detected something, there always was something, if only a possum or a cat. The few times I thought she was mistaken, I was proven wrong. Almost every time she detected a human interloper while I was asleep, she had him on the run before I was fully awake—not that she attacked, but she made a good show and he could not be sure she would not attack.

A few experiences like that and I think anyone would have to stop and think if forced to choose between his dog and his own arm. And I am not talking about a Lassie, a fictional dog who knows, somehow, to go for a doctor in case of illness and for the sheriff in case of criminals. I am talking about a rather ordinary dog doing as any ordinary dog might. To say I trusted Lizbeth in matters within her purview would hardly express it. Do I "trust" my fingers to hit some key (if not precisely the right one) as I type? After a while I relied on her without really noticing that I was. I did not hear with her ears, but I read the indications of what she heard from the fur on the back of her neck without having to think about it.

One morning we returned to a camp I had in a stand of bamboo. On my bedroll I found what appeared to be a snake. Yet my heart did not miss a beat. I knew instantly that whatever my eyes told me, it could not be a living snake because Lizbeth was utterly oblivious to it. Although I have explained it here, I did not have to reason it out at the time. I knew, and I knew as soon as I saw it. It proved to be a rubber toy snake that had been placed there by a malevolent companion. He was not in camp when I found the rubber snake, but afterward he laughed long and hard and said he wished he could have seen my reaction. He never did believe that there had been no reaction, so I too wish he had been there.

For her services as watchdog alone, Lizbeth was easily worth whatever extra trouble it was to keep her while I was on the streets. Beyond this, I know some of the help I received while I was on the streets is owing to Lizbeth. Some people clearly cared more for Lizbeth's welfare than my own. Several times I received unsolicited handouts that consisted only of dog food—this always happened when I still did have food for Lizbeth, but was going hungry myself. Many more people seemed to think I was trustworthy—or at least more worthy of assistance—because I had Lizbeth. I hesitate to write this, because as I do, it does seem rather likely that Lizbeth and I will be on the streets again, but I worry some about the welfare of people who trusted me only because I had a dog: A child molester, rapist, kidnapper, or serial killer could hardly do better than to have a dog as a lure and a cover.

Short of descending into pookum-ookums-snuggum-uggums, I can hardly overemphasize the psychological benefits I derived from having Lizbeth with me. Her companionship was worth something. Doggy companionship is no substitute for human companionship, not even for bad human companionship. But it is a great improvement over utter solitude.

Although I had no rural background, I had somehow absorbed the idea that one should care for the livestock before caring for oneself. For people who live by the animals they keep, of course, this principle is not a matter of unalloyed altruism, and it had its practical benefits for me. In caring for Lizbeth I cared for myself. In thinking of taking water to camp for her, I remembered to carry water for myself. Some times that I would not have done so otherwise, I went digging through the dumpsters to find something to feed her and turned up also something of value to myself. And nearly always I used the rationale of providing for her—later it was of providing for her and Clint—to deflect the humiliation and the shame so that I could do what I had to do.

For months at a time, Lizbeth and I were leash-length from each other almost constantly. Those times that we had been camping in a particular place with some regularity, she would soon learn the way to that place, and if because we were being observed, I wanted to avoid our secret path, she would invariably try to pull me toward our campsite. At first I supposed this meant she missed having a home. This was anthropomorphizing, and I paid for this error of thought in my feelings of guilt over not being able to provide her a home.

Yet she had her other habits, too. When we had been hitchhiking, for weeks afterward she thought any car that stopped nearby was stopped to give us a ride, and any open car door seemed to her to be an invitation to hop in. Eventually I began to see that her pulling toward our campsite was a habit of this sort. Within six months of our having left it, I had occasion to walk with Lizbeth past the shack on Avenue B, which had been home to her for more than two years after Jerry had passed a fifteen-dollar hot check to get the money to buy her. Yet Lizbeth was utterly indifferent to the place.

She did not know she was homeless. She did not know there was such a thing. She was dog. For all her dog brain knew, she was the dog of a hunter or a nomad. She was permitted to sleep behind her master's knee, and to lick his face in the morning. The truth was, most of the time she was perfectly happy, so far as a dog can be happy.

Now she greets Clint when he comes in. It is an elaborate routine. She tries to sit, because she knows this is something that pleases us sometimes, but she cannot contain the energy in her tail. She jumps and whirls and stands on her hind legs with her tongue extended, and will do it all again and again until Clint lets her lick his face.

She seems to know still that she is my dog—for when the thunder comes in the night, it's me she tries to crawl under. But she may be unsure whether it is Clint or I who is the alpha of the pack. At any rate, Clint's face has the particular advantage of being sweaty when he comes in. And sometimes Clint will take her for a little run, a run suitable for a dog her age—and this relieves a little of the boredom of being a writer's dog.

RICHARD FORD

Communist

M Y MOTHER ONCE had a boyfriend named Glen
Baxter. This was in 1961. We—my mother and I—
were living in the little house my father had left
her up the Sun River, near Victory, Montana, west of Great
Falls. My mother was thirty-two at the time. I was sixteen.
Glen Baxter was somewhere in the middle, between us,
though I cannot be exact about it.

We were living then off the proceeds of my father's life
insurance policies, with my mother doing some part-time
waitressing work up in Great Falls and going to the bars in
the evenings, which I know is where she met Glen Baxter.
Sometimes he would come back with her and stay in her
room at night, or she would call up from town and explain
that she was staying with him in his little place on Lewis
Street by the GN yards. She gave me his number every time,
but I never called it. I think she probably thought that what
she was doing was terrible, but simply couldn't help herself. I
thought it was all right, though. Regular life it seemed, and
still does. She was young, and I knew that even then.

Glen Baxter was a Communist and liked hunting, which
he talked about a lot. Pheasants. Ducks. Deer. He killed all of
them, he said. He had been to Vietnam as far back as then,

and when he was in our house he often talked about shooting the animals over there—monkeys and beautiful parrots—using military guns just for sport. We did not know what Vietnam was then, and Glen, when he talked about that, referred to it only as "the Far East." I think now he must've been in the CIA and been disillusioned by something he saw or found out about and been thrown out, but that kind of thing did not matter to us. He was a tall, dark-eyed man with short black hair, and was usually in a good humor. He had gone halfway through college in Peoria, Illinois, he said, where he grew up. But when he was around our life he worked wheat farms as a ditcher, and stayed out of work winters and in the bars drinking with women like my mother, who had work and some money. It is not an uncommon life to lead in Montana.

What I want to explain happened in November. We had not been seeing Glen Baxter for some time. Two months had gone by. My mother knew other men, but she came home most days from work and stayed inside watching television in her bedroom and drinking beers. I asked about Glen once, and she said only that she didn't know where he was, and I assumed they had had a fight and that he was gone off on a flyer back to Illinois or Massachusetts, where he said he had relatives. I'll admit that I liked him. He had something on his mind always. He was a labor man as well as a Communist, and liked to say that the country was poisoned by the rich, and strong men would need to bring it to life again, and I liked that because my father had been a labor man, which was why we had a house to live in and money coming through. It was also true that I'd had a few boxing bouts by then—just with town boys and one with an Indian from

Choteau—and there were some girlfriends I knew from that. I did not like my mother being around the house so much at night, and I wished Glen Baxter would come back, or that another man would come along and entertain her somewhere else.

At two o'clock on a Saturday, Glen drove up into our yard in a car. He had had a big brown Harley-Davidson that he rode most of the year, in his black-and-red irrigators and a baseball cap turned backwards. But this time he had a car, a blue Nash Ambassador. My mother and I went out on the porch when he stopped inside the olive trees my father had planted as a shelter belt, and my mother had a look on her face of not much pleasure. It was starting to be cold in earnest by then. Snow was down already onto the Fairfield Bench, though on this day a chinook was blowing, and it could as easily have been spring, though the sky above the Divide was turning over in silver and blue clouds of winter.

"We haven't seen you in a long time, I guess," my mother said coldly.

"My little retarded sister died," Glen said, standing at the door of his old car. He was wearing his orange VFW jacket and canvas shoes we called wino shoes, something I had never seen him wear before. He seemed to be in a good humor. "We buried her in Florida near the home."

"That's a good place," my mother said in a voice that meant she was a wronged party in something.

"I want to take this boy hunting today, Aileen," Glen said. "There're snow geese down now. But we have to go right away, or they'll be gone to Idaho by tomorrow."

"He doesn't care to go," my mother said.

"Yes I do," I said, and looked at her.

My mother frowned at me. "Why do you?"

"Why does he need a reason?" Glen Baxter said and grinned.

"I want him to have one, that's why." She looked at me oddly. "I think Glen's drunk, Les."

"No, I'm not drinking," Glen said, which was hardly ever true. He looked at both of us, and my mother bit down on the side of her lower lip and stared at me in a way to make you think she thought something was being put over on her and she didn't like you for it. She was very pretty, though when she was mad her features were sharpened and less pretty by a long way. "All right, then I don't care," she said to no one in particular. "Hunt, kill, maim. Your father did that too." She turned to go back inside.

"Why don't you come with us, Aileen?" Glen was smiling still, pleased.

"To do what?" my mother said. She stopped and pulled a package of cigarettes out of her dress pocket and put one in her mouth.

"It's worth seeing."

"See dead animals?" my mother said.

"These geese are from Siberia, Aileen," Glen said. "They're not like a lot of geese. Maybe I'll buy us dinner later. What do you say?"

"Buy what with?" my mother said. To tell the truth, I didn't know why she was so mad at him. I would've thought she'd be glad to see him. But she just suddenly seemed to hate everything about him.

"I've got some money," Glen said. "Let me spend it on a pretty girl tonight."

"Find one of those and you're lucky," my mother said, turning away toward the front door.

"I already found one," Glen Baxter said. But the door slammed behind her, and he looked at me then with a look I think now was helplessness, though I could not see a way to change anything.

My mother sat in the backseat of Glen's Nash and looked out the window while we drove. My double gun was in the seat between us beside Glen's Belgian pump, which he kept loaded with five shells in case, he said, he saw something beside the road he wanted to shoot. I had hunted rabbits before, and had ground-sluiced pheasants and other birds, but I had never been on an actual hunt before, one where you drove out to some special place and did it formally. And I was excited. I had a feeling that something important was about to happen to me, and that this would be a day I would always remember.

My mother did not say anything for a long time, and neither did I. We drove up through Great Falls and out the other side toward Fort Benton, which was on the benchland where wheat was grown.

"Geese mate for life," my mother said, just out of the blue, as we were driving. "I hope you know that. They're special birds."

"I know that," Glen said in the front seat. "I have every respect for them."

"So where were you for three months?" she said. "I'm only curious."

"I was in the Big Hole for a while," Glen said, "and after that I went over to Douglas, Wyoming."

"What were you planning to do there?" my mother asked.

"I wanted to find a job, but it didn't work out."

"I'm going to college," she said suddenly, and this was something I had never heard about before. I turned to look at her, but she was staring out her window and wouldn't see me.

"I knew French once," Glen said. "*Rosé*'s pink. *Rouge*'s red." He glanced at me and smiled. "I think that's a wise idea, Aileen. When are you going to start?"

"I don't want Les to think he was raised by crazy people all his life," my mother said.

"Les ought to go himself," Glen said.

"After I go, he will."

"What do you say about that, Les?" Glen said, grinning.

"He says it's just fine," my mother said.

"It's just fine," I said.

Where Glen Baxter took us was out onto the high flat prairie that was disked for wheat and had high, high mountains out to the east, with lower heartbreak hills in between. It was, I remember, a day for blues in the sky, and down in the distance we could see the small town of Floweree, and the state highway running past it toward Fort Benton and the Hi-line. We drove out on top of the prairie on a muddy dirt road fenced on both sides, until we had gone about three miles, which is where Glen stopped.

"All right," he said, looking up in the rearview mirror at my mother. "You wouldn't think there was anything here, would you?"

"*We're* here," my mother said. "You brought us here."

"You'll be glad though," Glen said, and seemed confident to me. I had looked around myself but could not see anything. No water or trees, nothing that seemed like a good place to hunt anything. Just wasted land. "There's a big lake out there, Les," Glen said. "You can't see it now from here because it's low. But the geese are there. You'll see."

"It's like the moon out here, I recognize that," my mother said, "only it's worse." She was staring out at the flat wheatland as if she could actually see something in particular, and wanted to know more about it. "How'd you find this place?"

"I came once on a wheat push," Glen said.

"And I'm sure the owner told you just to come back and hunt anytime you like and bring anybody you wanted. Come one, come all. Is that it?"

"People shouldn't own land anyway," Glen said. "Anybody should be able to use it."

"Les, Glen's going to poach here," my mother said. "I just want you to know that, because that's a crime and the law will get you for it. If you're a man now, you're going to have to face the consequences."

"That's not true," Glen Baxter said, and looked gloomily out over the steering wheel down the muddy road toward the mountains. Though for myself I believed it was true, and didn't care. I didn't care about anything at that moment except seeing geese fly over me and shooting them down.

"Well, I'm certainly not going out there," my mother said. "I like towns better, and I already have enough trouble."

"That's okay," Glen said. "When the geese lift up you'll get to see them. That's all I wanted. Les and me'll go shoot them, won't we, Les?"

"Yes," I said, and I put my hand on my shotgun, which had been my father's and was heavy as rocks.

"Then we should go on," Glen said, "or we'll waste our light."

We got out of the car with our guns. Glen took off his canvas shoes and put on his pair of black irrigators out of the trunk. Then we crossed the barbed wire fence, and walked out into the high, tilled field toward nothing. I looked back at my mother when we were still not so far away, but I could only see the small, dark top of her head, low in the backseat of the Nash, starting out and thinking what I could not then begin to say.

On the walk toward the lake, Glen began talking to me. I had never been alone with him, and knew little about him except what my mother said—that he drank too much, or other times that he was the nicest man she had ever known in the world and that someday a woman would marry him, though she didn't think it would be her. Glen told me as we walked that he wished he had finished college, but that it was too late now, that his mind was too old. He said he had liked the Far East very much, and that people there knew how to treat each other, and that he would go back some day but couldn't go now. He said also that he would like to live in Russia for a while and mentioned the names of people who had gone there, names I didn't know. He said it would be hard at first, because it was so different, but that pretty soon anyone would learn to like it and wouldn't want to live anywhere else, and that Russians treated Americans who came to live there like kings. There were Communists everywhere now, he said. You didn't know them, but they were there.

Montana had a large number, and he was in touch with all of them. He said that Communists were always in danger and that he had to protect himself all the time. And when he said that he pulled back his VFW jacket and showed me the butt of a pistol he had stuck under his shirt against his bare skin. "There are people who want to kill me right now," he said, "and I would kill a man myself if I thought I had to." And we kept walking. Though in a while he said, "I don't think I know much about you, Les. But I'd like to. What do you like to do?"

"I like to box," I said. "My father did it. It's a good thing to know."

"I suppose you have to protect yourself too," Glen said.

"I know how to," I said.

"Do you like to watch TV," Glen asked, and smiled.

"Not much."

"I love to," Glen said. "I could watch it instead of eating if I had one."

I looked out straight ahead over the green tops of sage that grew to the edge of the disked field, hoping to see the lake Glen said was there. There was an airishness and a sweet smell that I thought might be the place we were going, but I couldn't see it. "How will we hunt these geese?" I said.

"It won't be hard," Glen said. "Most hunting isn't even hunting. It's only shooting. And that's what this will be. In Illinois you would dig holes in the ground and hide and set out your decoys. Then the geese come to you, over and over again. But we don't have time for that here." He glanced at me. "You have to be sure the first time here."

"How do you know they're here now," I asked. And I looked toward the Highwood Mountains twenty miles away, half in snow and half dark blue at the bottom. I could see the little town of Floweree then, looking shabby and dimly lighted in the distance. A red bar sign shone. A car moved slowly away from the scattered buildings.

"They always come November first," Glen said.

"Are we going to poach them?"

"Does it make any difference to you," Glen asked.

"No, it doesn't."

"Well then, we aren't," he said.

We walked then for a while without talking. I looked back once to see the Nash far and small in the flat distance. I couldn't see my mother, and I thought that she must've turned on the radio and gone to sleep, which she always did, letting it play all night in her bedroom. Behind the car the sun was nearing the rounded mountains southwest of us, and I knew that when the sun was gone it would be cold. I wished my mother had decided to come along with us, and I thought for a moment of how little I really knew her at all.

Glen walked with me another quarter-mile, crossed another barbed wire fence where sage was growing, then went a hundred yards through wheatgrass and spurge until the ground went up and formed a kind of long hillock bunker built by a farmer against the wind. And I realized the lake was just beyond us. I could hear the sound of a car horn blowing and a dog barking all the way down in the town, then the wind seemed to move and all I could hear then and after then were geese. So many geese, from the sound of them, though I still could not see even one. I stood and listened to the high-pitched shouting sound, a sound I had never heard so close, a sound with size to it—though it was not loud. A sound that meant great numbers and that made your chest rise and your shoulders tighten with expectancy. It was a sound to make you feel separate from it and everything else, as if you were of no importance in the grand scheme of things.

"Do you hear them singing," Glen asked. He held his hand up to make me stand still. And we both listened. "How many do you think, Les, just hearing?"

"A hundred," I said. "More than a hundred."

"Five thousand," Glen said. "More than you can believe when you see them. Go see."

I put down my gun and on my hands and knees crawled up the earthwork through the wheatgrass and thistle, until I could see down to the lake and see the geese. And they were there, like a white bandage laid on the water, wide and long and continuous, a white expanse of snow geese, seventy yards from me, on the bank, but stretching far onto the lake, which was large itself—a half-mile across, with thick tules on the far side and wild plums farther and the blue mountain behind them.

"Do you see the big raft?" Glen said from below me, in a whisper.

"I see it," I said, still looking. It was such a thing to see, a view I had never seen and have not since.

"Are any on the land?" he said.

"Some are in the wheatgrass," I said, "but most are swimming."

"Good," Glen said. "They'll have to fly. But we can't wait for that now."

And I crawled backwards down the heel of land to where Glen was, and my gun. We were losing our light, and the air was purplish and cooling. I looked toward the car but couldn't see it, and I was no longer sure where it was below the lighted sky.

"Where do they fly to?" I said in a whisper, since I did not want anything to be ruined because of what I did or said. It was important to Glen to shoot the geese, and it was important to me.

"To the wheat," he said. "Or else they leave for good. I wish your mother had come, Les. Now she'll be sorry."

I could hear the geese quarreling and shouting on the lake surface. And I wondered if they knew we were here now. "She might be," I said with my heart pounding, but I didn't think she would be much.

It was a simple plan he had. I would stay behind the bunker, and he would crawl on his belly with his gun through the wheatgrass as near to the geese as he could. Then he would simply stand up and shoot all the ones he could close up, both in the air and on the ground. And when all the others flew up, with luck some would turn toward me as they came into the wind, and then I could shoot them and turn them back to him, and he would shoot them again. He could kill ten, he said, if he was lucky, and I might kill four. It didn't seem hard.

"Don't show them your face," Glen said. "Wait till you think you can touch them, then stand up and shoot. To hesitate is lost in this."

"All right," I said. "I'll try it."

"Shoot one in the head, and then shoot another one," Glen said. "It won't be hard." He patted me on the arm and smiled. Then he took off his VFW jacket and put it on the ground, climbed up the side of the bunker, cradling his shotgun in his arms, and slid on his belly into the dry stalks of yellow grass out of my sight.

Then, for the first time in that entire day, I was alone. And I didn't mind it. I sat squat down in the grass, loaded my double gun and took my other two shells out of my pocket to hold. I pushed the safety off and on to see that it was right. The wind rose a little, scuffed the grass and made me shiver. It was not the warm chinook now, but a wind out of the north, the one geese flew away from if they could.

Then I thought about my mother, in the car alone, and how much longer I would stay with her, and what it might mean to her for me to leave. And I wondered when Glen Baxter would die and if someone would kill him, or whether my mother would marry him and how I would feel about it. And though I didn't know why, it occurred to me that Glen Baxter and I would not be friends when all was said and done, since I didn't care if he ever married my mother or didn't.

Then I thought about boxing and what my father had taught me about it. To tighten your fists hard. To strike out straight from the shoulder and never punch backing up. How to cut a punch by snapping your fist inwards, how to carry your chin low, and to step toward a man when he is falling so you can hit him again. And most important, to keep your eyes open when you are hitting in the face and causing damage, because you need to see what you're doing to encourage yourself, and because it is when you close your eyes that you stop hitting and get hurt badly. "Fly all over your man, Les," my father said. "When you see your chance, fly on him and hit him till he falls." That, I thought, would always be my attitude in things.

And then I heard the geese again, their voices in unison, louder and shouting, as if the wind had changed again and put all new sounds in the cold air. And then a *boom*. And I knew Glen was in among them and had stood up to shoot. The noise of geese rose and grew worse, and my fingers burned where I held my gun too tight to the metal, and I put it down and opened my fist to make the burning stop so I could feel the trigger when the moment came. *Boom*, Glen shot again, and I heard him shuck a shell, and all the sounds out beyond the bunker seemed to be rising—the geese, the shots, the air itself going up. *Boom*, Glen shot another time, and I knew he was taking his careful time to make his shots good. And I held my gun and started to crawl up the bunker so as not to be surprised when the geese came over me and I could shoot.

From the top I saw Glen Baxter alone in the wheatgrass field, shooting at a white goose with black tips of wings that was on the ground not far from him, but trying to run and pull into the air. He shot it once more, and it fell over dead with its wings flapping.

Glen looked back at me and his face was distorted and strange. The air around him was full of white rising geese and he seemed to want them all. "Behind you, Les," he yelled at me and pointed. "They're all behind you now." I looked behind me, and there were geese in the air as far as I could see, more than I knew how many, moving so slowly, their wings wide out and working calmly and filling the air with noise, though their voices were not as loud or as shrill as I had thought they would be. And they were so close! Forty feet, some of them. The air around me vibrated and I could feel the wind from their wings and it seemed to me I could kill as many as the times I could shoot—a hundred or a thousand—and I raised my gun, put the muzzle on the head of a white goose, and fired. It shuddered in the air, its wide feet sank below its belly, its wings cradled out to hold back air, and it fell straight down and landed with an awful sound, a noise a human would make, a thick, soft, *hump* noise. I looked up again and shot another goose, could hear the pellets hit its chest, but it didn't fall or even break its pattern for flying. *Boom*, Glen shot again. And then again. "Hey," I heard him shout, "Hey, hey." And there were geese flying over me, flying in line after line. I broke my gun and reloaded, and thought to myself as I did: I need confidence here, I need to be sure with this. I pointed at another goose and shot it in the head, and it fell the way the first one had, wings out, its belly down, and with the same thick noise of hitting. Then I sat down in the grass on the bunker and let geese fly over me.

By now the whole raft was in the air, all of it moving in a slow swirl above me and the lake and everywhere, finding the wind and heading out south in long wavering lines that caught the last sun and turned to silver as they gained a distance. It was a thing to see, I will tell you now. Five thousand white geese all in the air around you, making a noise like you have never heard before. And I thought to myself then: this is something I will never see again. I will never forget this. And I was right.

Glen Baxter shot twice more. One he missed, but with the other he hit a goose flying away from him, and knocked it half falling and flying into the empty lake not far from shore, where it began to swim as though it was fine and make its noise.

Glen stood in the stubby grass, looking out at the goose, his gun lowered. "I didn't need to shoot that one, did I, Les?"

"I don't know," I said, sitting on the little knoll of land, looking at the goose swimming in the water.

"I don't know why I shoot 'em. They're so beautiful." He looked at me.

"I don't know either," I said.

"Maybe there's nothing else to do with them." Glen stared at the goose again and shook his head. "Maybe this is exactly what they're put on earth for."

I did not know what to say because I did not know what he could mean by that, though what I felt was embarrassment at the great numbers of geese there were, and a dulled feeling like a hunger because the shooting had stopped and it was over for me now.

Glen began to pick up his geese, and I walked down to my two that had fallen close together and were dead. One had hit with such an impact that its stomach had split and some of its inward parts were knocked out. Though the other looked unhurt, its soft white belly turned up like a pillow, its head and jagged bill-teeth, its tiny black eyes looking as they would if they were alive.

"What's happened to the hunters out here?" I heard a voice speak. It was my mother, standing in her pink dress on the knoll above us, hugging her arms. She was smiling though she was cold. And I realized that I had lost all thought of her in the shooting. "Who did all this shooting? Is this your work, Les?"

"No," I said.

"Les is a hunter, though, Aileen," Glen said. "He takes his time." He was holding two white geese by their necks, one in each hand, and he was smiling. He and my mother seemed pleased.

"I see you didn't miss too many," my mother said and smiled. I could tell she admired Glen for his geese, and that she had done some thinking in the car alone. "It *was* wonderful, Glen," she said. "I've never seen anything like that. They were like snow."

"It's worth seeing once, isn't it?" Glen said. "I should've killed more, but I got excited."

My mother looked at me then. "Where's yours, Les?"

"Here," I said and pointed to my two geese on the ground beside me.

My mother nodded in a nice way, and I think she liked everything then and wanted the day to turn out right and for all of us to be happy. "Six, then. You've got six in all."

"One's still out there," I said, and motioned where the one goose was swimming in circles on the water.

"Okay," my mother said and put her hand over her eyes to look. "Where is it?"

Glen Baxter looked at me then with a strange smile, a smile that said he wished I had never mentioned anything about the other goose. And I wished I hadn't either. I looked up in the sky and could see the lines of geese by the thousands shining silver in the light, and I wished we could just leave and go home.

"That one's my mistake there," Glen Baxter said and grinned. "I shouldn't have shot that one, Aileen. I got too excited."

My mother looked out on the lake for a minute, then looked at Glen and back again. "Poor goose." She shook her head. "How will you get it, Glen?"

"I can't get that one now," Glen said.

My mother looked at him. "What do you mean?"

"I'm going to leave that one," Glen said.

"Well, no. You can't leave one," my mother said. "You shot it. You have to get it. Isn't that a rule?"

"No," Glen said.

And my mother looked from Glen to me. "Wade out and get it, Glen," she said in a sweet way, and my mother looked young then, like a young girl, in her flimsy short-sleeved waitress dress and her skinny, bare legs in the wheatgrass.

"No." Glen Baxter looked down at his gun and shook his head. And I didn't know why he wouldn't go, because it would've been easy. The lake was shallow. And you could tell that anyone could've walked out a long way before it got deep, and Glen had on his boots.

My mother looked at the white goose, which was not more than thirty yards from the shore, its head up, moving in slow circles, its wings settled and relaxed so you could see the black tips. "Wade out and get it, Glenny, won't you, please?" she said. "They're special things."

"You don't understand the world, Aileen," Glen said. "This can happen. It doesn't matter."

"But that's so cruel, Glen," she said, and a sweet smile came on her lips.

"Raise up your own arms, 'Leeny," Glen said. "I can't see any angel's wings, can you Les?" He looked at me, but I looked away.

"Then you go on and get it, Les," my mother said. "You weren't raised by crazy people." I started to go, but Glen Baxter suddenly grabbed me by my shoulder and pulled me back hard, so hard his fingers made bruises in my skin that I saw later.

"Nobody's going," he said. "This is over with now."

And my mother gave Glen a cold look then. "You don't have a heart, Glen," she said. "There's nothing to love in you. You're just a son of a bitch, that's all."

And Glen Baxter nodded at my mother, then, as if he understood something he had not understood before, but something that he was willing to know. "Fine," he said, "that's fine." And he took his big pistol out from against his belly, the big blue revolver I had only seen part of before and that he said protected him, and he pointed it out at the goose on the water, his arm straight away from him, and shot and missed. And then he shot and missed again. The goose made its noise once. And then he hit it dead, because there was no splash. And then he shot it three times more until the gun was empty and the goose's head was down and it was floating toward the middle of the lake where it was empty and dark blue. "Now who has a heart?" Glen said. But my mother was not there when he turned around. She had already started back to the car and was almost lost from sight in the darkness. And Glen smiled at me then and his face had a wild look on it. "Okay, Les?" he said.

"Okay," I said.

"There're limits to everything, right?"

"I guess so," I said.

"Your mother's a beautiful woman, but she's not the only beautiful woman in Montana." And I did not say anything. And Glen Baxter suddenly said, "Here," and he held the pistol out at me. "Don't you want this? Don't you want to shoot me? Nobody thinks they'll die. But I'm ready for it right now." And I did not know what to do then. Though it is true that what I wanted to do was to hit him, hit him as hard in the face as I could, and see him on the ground bleeding and crying and pleading for me to stop. Only at that moment he looked scared to me, and I had never seen a grown man scared before—though I have seen one since—and I felt sorry for him, as though he was already a dead man. And I did not end up hitting him at all.

A light can go out in the heart. All of this happened years ago, but I still can feel now how sad and remote the world was to me. Glen Baxter, I think now, was not a bad man, only a man scared of something he'd never seen before—something soft in himself—his life going a way he didn't like. A woman with a son. Who could blame him there? I don't know what makes people do what they do, or call themselves what they call themselves, only that you have to live someone's life to be the expert.

My mother had tried to see the good side of things, tried to be hopeful in the situation she was handed, tried to look out for us both, and it hadn't worked. It was a strange time in her life then and after that, a time when she had to adjust to being an adult just when she was on the thin edge of things. Too much awareness too early in life was her problem, I think.

And what I felt was only that I had somehow been pushed out into the world, into the real life then, the one I hadn't lived yet. In a year I was gone to hard-rock mining and no-paycheck jobs and not to college. And I have thought more than once about my mother saying that I had not been raised by crazy people, and I don't know what that could mean or what difference it could make, unless it means that love is a reliable commodity, and even that is not always true, as I have found out.

Late on the night that all this took place I was in bed when I heard my mother say, "Come outside, Les. Come and hear this." And I went out onto the front porch barefoot and in my underwear, where it was warm like spring, and there was a spring mist in the air. I could see the lights of the Fairfield Coach in the distance, on its way up to Great Falls.

And I could hear geese, white birds in the sky, flying. They made their high-pitched sound like angry yells, and though I couldn't see them high up, it seemed to me they were everywhere. And my mother looked up and said, "Hear them?" I could smell her hair wet from the shower. "They leave with the moon," she said. "It's still half wild out here."

And I said, "I hear them," and I felt a chill come over my bare chest, and the hair stood up on my arms the way it does before a storm. And for a while we listened.

"When I first married your father, you know, we lived on a street called Bluebird Canyon, in California. And I thought that was the prettiest street and the prettiest name. I suppose no one brings you up like your first love. You don't mind if I say that, do you?" She looked at me hopefully.

"No," I said.

"We have to keep civilization alive somehow." And she pulled her little housecoat together because there was a cold vein in the air, a part of the cold that would be on us the next day. "I don't feel part of things tonight, I guess."

"It's all right," I said.

"Do you know where I'd like to go?"

"No," I said. And I suppose I knew she was angry then, angry with life, but did not want to show me that.

"To the Straits of Juan de Fuca. Wouldn't that be something? Would you like that?"

"I'd like it," I said. And my mother looked off for a minute, as if she could see the Straits of Juan de Fuca out against the line of mountains, see the lights of things alive and a whole new world.

"I know you liked him," she said after a moment. "You and I both suffer fools too well."

"I didn't like him too much," I said. "I didn't really care."

"He'll fall on his face. I'm sure of that," she said. And I didn't say anything because I didn't care about Glen Baxter anymore, and was happy not to talk about him. "Would you tell me something if I asked you? Would you tell me the truth?"

"Yes," I said.

And my mother did not look at me. "Just tell the truth," she said.

"All right," I said.

"Do you think I'm still very feminine? I'm thirty-two years old now. You don't know what that means. But do you think I am?"

And I stood at the edge of the porch, with the olive trees before me, looking straight up into the mist where I could not see geese but could still hear them flying, could almost feel the air move below their white wings. And I felt the way you feel when you are on a trestle all alone and the train is coming, and you know you have to decide. And I said, "Yes, I do." Because that was the truth. And I tried to think of something else then and did not hear what my mother said after that.

And how old was I then? Sixteen. Sixteen is young, but it can also be a grown man. I am forty-one years old now, and I think about that time without regret, though my mother and I never talked in that way again, and I have not heard her voice now in a long, long time.

JANET HAMILL

The Birds of the Air

L ONG AFTER THE tower bells called the monks to their devotions the ringing echoed in Brother Hugo's ears. It was a sensation unlike any he'd known in Paris, where even the bells of Notre Dame could be drowned in the city din—swine, sheep, and cattle led in noisy numbers through muddy streets, the swift gallop of horses, hawking merchants, whining beggars, the near-hysterical pitch of crowds on holy days, and above it all, the incessant verbal jousting of the men of the university—rowdy scholars and bands of students joking and drinking, quarreling and shouting, in constant debate. In the college corridors, in the streets and taverns Hugo walked among them, partaking of the mental feast; and sometimes in the middle of a labyrinthine argument, when lowering his voice to mark a fine point of logic, he'd regard their rapt, embattled faces and laugh uproariously.

All those discordant sounds were miles away from the shady arcades of the Abbey of Saint-Michel-De-Cuxa. There Brother Hugo walked in procession to chapel wondering when, if ever, he'd achieve the spiritual serenity he sought in monastic life. For try as he may, since he'd been at the abbey, he couldn't keep his thoughts on God. The bells, the interludes of silence, the daily round of meals, the light at sunset, and the music of the psalms kept taking him back to the world he'd left behind—a world of heady ideas with scholars embroiled in intellectual controversy; a turbulent world where philosophical war was waged between the claims of faith and reason in the wake of recent translations into Latin of Aristotle's corpus.

Surrounded by his fellow monks with bowed, hooded heads before the chapel crucifix, Brother Hugo brooded on the atmosphere of intolerance and enmity that developed in his last days in Paris—where iron dogma and a perverse form of reason without heart fought for his allegiance. The collegial spirit was waning amidst the bitter polemic and the joys of scholarship and instruction dimmed in the dark political wrangle. It was an insufferable atmosphere in which Hugo was torn between staying on at the university or leaving. And to help him make a decision, he prayed to his patron saint for a sign.

One sleepless night it came. A fruit tree densely covered with white blossoms appeared before him at the foot of his bed. The vision grew large and he saw that it was birds, not blossoms, covering the branches. One bird alighted from the tree and flew over a road winding out of his window into the distance. The flight drew him up from his bed with an incredible urge to follow the bird. And from that moment Brother Hugo knew he'd be leaving Paris.

The Abbey of Saint-Michel-De-Cuxa was a self-sufficient Benedictine enclave set in a quiet forest valley in the Pyrenees. Under the leadership of its abbot, Oliva, its library had become celebrated throughout France, and for that reason Hugo chose the abbey as his refuge. In time, through the daily practice of his monastic duties, safe in an oasis of sanctity, he forgot the tumult of the world he'd left behind and turned his thoughts to God. Four hours a day he prayed to God the Father, the Son, and the Holy Ghost, for the souls of the living and the souls of the dead, and never before did the mysteries of his faith seem more profound.

Because he'd been a university scholar the Benedictine Order required Hugo to perform the specific duties of teaching in the abbey school and copying manuscripts. But when duty allowed, at Oliva's urging, he made use of the library's volumes of Plato, Augustine, and Boethius and wrote tractates on the Trinity and the Incarnation.

In spring and summer when days were longer he tended the gardens and orchards, feeling closest there to God among the olive trees, palms, fig trees, cypress, and grape vines lining the groves around the abbey; the iris, myrtle, herbs, and apple trees of the cloister garden; the spiders, bees, and butterflies; the fish in the fountain; and the larks, thrushes, wrens, and swallows whose continual singing was to him a melodious prayer.

Making use of his scientific learning, Brother Hugo filled notebooks with manifold observations of nature in the gardens and orchards. He described an apple from peel to core. He illustrated in detail the leaves of every tree and plant. He observed spiders spinning their webs and leaping on their prey, the entire honey-making process of bees, and the emergence of birds from eggs.

Oliva praised the scientific observations and welcomed the notebooks as an addition to the library because he believed, as Hugo did, that men could best understand their

Creator once they understood in full the nature of His creations.

But Brother Hugo's happy, productive years at Saint-Michel-De-Cuxa came to an end. One chilly autumn night the abbot died in his sleep from the multiple woes of old age. Within weeks of Oliva's passing, the Benedictines appointed Ambrose of Arles to succeed him.

The new abbot, who arrived with an entourage more suitable to a noble than a clergyman, was an ardent and sanctimonious man who saw himself as a church reformer. He was unread in the classics and philosophy. He had no sympathy for the new ideas coming from the cathedral schools and universities. And he believed that nature was the work of God and it wasn't man's place to inquire into the conundrums of the material world created by Him.

To purge the abbey of his predecessor's "corruptions," the new abbot padlocked the library and banned the reading of anything other than Holy Scripture. And because Hugo, more than any other monk, was to Ambrose the embodiment of Oliva's "decadent reign" he forbade him to teach and assigned him to twelve hours a day of manual labor.

Once again Brother Hugo found himself weighed down with melancholy, praying to his patron saint for a sign that would help him decide his future.

One sleepless night it came. A fruit tree densely covered with white blossoms appeared before him in his cell. The vision grew large and he saw that it was birds, not blossoms, covering the branches. One bird alighted from the tree and flew over a road winding out of his window into the distance. The flight drew him up from his bed with an incredible urge to follow the bird. And from that moment he knew he'd be leaving the abbey.

Early Christmas morning while the abbey slept, Brother Hugo left the walls of Saint-Michel-De-Cuxa and set out on the pilgrim road to Compostela. He took nothing with him but his sandals, the grey and white robe he wore, a wooden rosary, and a beggar's wallet. Though it was his ostensible goal, it wasn't necessary that he reach the Apostle James's shrine in western Spain. He was simply retiring from the world.

That winter the Pyrenees were particularly dangerous, but Hugo refused to be impeded by the deep snow and threat of avalanches. With each step he was retreating further and further into his solitude. Sustained by the generosity of the churches and hospices along the way, by spring he reached the swollen banks of the Aragon, a small tributary of the Ebro River north of Saragossa.

It was nightfall as Brother Hugo stood on the eastern shore, wondering whether to wait until morning to make his crossing. And as he stood and wondered, a little bird appeared and hovered over his head. The bird flew to the other side of the stream, then back to Hugo. He made the same flight a second time, and the third time Hugo followed him.

Having crossed the narrow but swollen tributary, Brother Hugo was exhausted and lay down on the shore. But the little bird wouldn't let him rest. He flew into the nearby woods, then back to Brother Hugo, perching on his head. He made the same flight a second time, and the third time Hugo pulled himself up from the ground and followed him.

With a full moon overhead, the little bird and Brother

Hugo went deep into the forest, coming to a stop in a clearing. There beneath a circular canopy of towering pines was an abandoned hut. The little bird flew in through the open doorway, and Hugo followed him. But for a crude table, a stool, and a straw pallet the hut was empty.

Through a window on the rear wall Hugo saw a fruit tree densely covered with white blossoms. He stood closer to the window and saw that it was birds, not blossoms, covering the branches—hundreds of birds, whose singing was like a heavenly choir. When he opened the window to better hear the birds, they flew into the hut and sat on his head and shoulders in such numbers that he laughed uproariously.

GARY INDIANA

A Bird Left Out of Literature

W HEN I WAS writing my book about J., years ago, certain animals kept slipping into the story as metaphors, bats for example, because J. was a night creature, and possessed a sort of radar for finding the places he needed to go. He was like an animal who had adapted, tenaciously, to a vanishing habitat, attracting the necessities of life by a combination of cleverness and over-powering beauty, but incapable of surviving a small, drastic change in the environment—I do not know exactly when J. contracted HIV since as late as a year before his death he claimed to have tested negative.

I lived for a while in a farmhouse in Tuscany, with no electricity. My absent host had spent little time there since the end of his first marriage. The house was full of objects that evoked that marriage—cameras, books, trunks of old clothes, his drawing board, her tripod, a box of crumbling pastels, a stash of Havana cigars. These physical reminders of how other people lived—with houses and cars and lives in common, pleasure trips, work—made my long affair with J., which had no such residua, seem ephemeral, a charged block of time that would vanish completely unless I wrote about it. At dusk the sky filled with wheeling black motes, like swarms of giant flies. As darkness settled in, single bats swooped near the house, bolts of black lightning, gorging on moths and mosquitoes.

I wrote my book about J. every night on a manual typewriter, by the dim light of a kerosene lamp. The typewriter ribbon was drastically faded, even ripped in spots, and certain keys jammed together; the mechanical difficulty of getting a paragraph written probably convinced me that I was writing well. The lamp attracted a fantastic profusion of bugs, which at first annoyed me and then gave me a welcomely distracting spectacle. A case of new wine had been delivered by a mysterious stranger from Pescara, the kind of weak domestic product you can drink all night with almost no effect. When I had finished squeezing the day's words out of myself, usually around midnight, I opened a fresh bottle and watched the insects gather on the writing table: moths, lacewings, planthoppers, all sorts of winged and unwinged creatures. I did not know what most of them were. Oddly, each bug seemed indifferent to all the others; they didn't fight, or eat each other. Nor did they crawl or flit about much. They simply settled on a spot and kept to it, barely moving.

I knew while I wrote my book about J. that my youth was ending. The things that had always tormented me would either change or not change, but writing the book made them completely visible, finally. The months I spent alone in the farmhouse were weighted with melancholy. I liked that the house was ancient and crumbling and vulnerable to scorpions and vipers, though the one time a viper actually appeared—an enormous one—I went scrambling on my moped to find the local shepherd, who killed it with a pitchfork.

There was no anti-venom kit in the house, and none to be had in the village; tales of viper death were a favorite staple of the village's one café, but when you questioned people closely, these fatalities moved further and further back in time. Maybe someone in 1900 had been killed by a viper, maybe not.

I took the train to Florence one week to visit friends. I had trouble finding their apartment, and almost returned to the farm without seeing them. The farm's isolation had practically robbed me of speech. This book, this terrible book, I kept saying—and my friends, whose atelier in Germany had hosted the writing of an earlier draft of the same book, assured me that I would, one day, finish it. They too were in the grip of work that seemed impossible to finish, and yet they knew it would come to an end sooner or later; it had to: they could only do the work in Prato, and their sublease was up in October.

I bought books in Florence, works of natural history, philosophical encyclopedias, a biography of Leibnitz, novels. I read up on bats. I learned that many rain forests are pollinated by bats. Without bats entire ecosystems would die off. Bats—I heard myself telling some bat-phobic acquaintance —aren't any sort of rodent. They're essential to the control of insects. They are much cleaner than most birds. They do not attack humans; like most animals, they're afraid of us. Nor do they carry rabies. A tiny number of bats acquire rabies, but die of it almost immediately. Unlike other animals, bats don't become aggressive when they are rabid.

Nearly all North American and European bat species are insectivorous. They're among the gentlest, most timid creatures in nature. They do not get tangled in hair. They have

excellent eyesight. Vast populations of nesting bats are exterminated by oafs and rednecks who set off cherry bombs and
fire rifles into bat caves, crippling the animals' echolocation.

I couldn't convey all this bat knowledge to the local
farmers, who detested bats, since my grasp of the Tuscan dialect amounted to nothing. The farmers were precisely the
kind of ignorant oafs who enjoy killing small, defenseless
creatures, the kind of oafs the human race produces in suicidal abundance. Evenings in the village were only slightly less
morbid than sitting alone with a bottle of bad wine watching
moths accumulate on my manuscript: there was nothing at
all charming about the local people, who seemed to do nothing but drink, play cards, and stare into the distance. One
majestic sunset followed another, the same terrible coffee
was served, the same moronic jokes were told. Meanwhile
my book, as I read through it, struck me as a gross, mis-
shapen effort, distorted in the wrong direction, a regular
abortion . . .

At the end of that curious period, the stranger from
Pescara, a fabulously wealthy woman who wanted me to
meet her protegé, an artist-industrialist, shanghaied me to
Piedmont, to another farm, and after some days there I went
to Turin, from Turin to Milan. From Milan I accompanied
an American art dealer to Cologne, learning en route that
she had neglected to reserve a hotel room for me, and had
also failed to book my flight to New York, things she'd
promised to do weeks earlier. Stranded and unwelcome in
the upstairs rooms of a gallery where a turd-like bronze by
Joseph Beuys was being merchandised for $1.5 million, I de-
cided to go for a walk. On the sidewalk, I ran directly into D.,
with whom I had had, three years earlier, the second most

miserable affair of my life. We looked at each other in horror, then walked away from each other at a gallop. I retrieved my luggage from the gallery and fled to the train station.

In Paris, I once again read through my book about J. and realized that everything in it was wrong, phony, sentimental, unbelievable. I ripped the whole thing to shreds and flushed the pieces down the toilet. This took several hours, as the water pressure on the rue Vieille du Temple provided only one full flush every twenty minutes or so. Once the manuscript had become one with the Paris sewer system, I felt liberated for several days. I treated myself to oysters at La Coupole. I decided never to return to New York. I'd start an entirely new life in Paris. How would I make a living? Well, I could . . .

. . . not do anything, really. I had no special skills, my French was terrible. I had nothing else to do in my life except start the book all over again, not that it would solve anything. So I resumed the story of J., which had formed a dense, hard core of congealed emotions inside me. I did not stick to the truth, exactly, because many things that had happened with J. were too bizarre to be believed. Reality, when I wrote it down, did not have the ring of reality. Who would believe, for example, that after months of intimate daily contact with a heroin addict, I continued to believe his prevarications, his lies, his outright denials that he was on heroin? That he could, on one occasion, exhibit an unbelievable mood swing, from the depths of suicidal despair to a sort of goofy optimism, after visiting a restaurant toilet during breakfast, and then, in tones of profound revelation, confide that he suffered from hypoglycemia?

The last time I saw J.—well, not the very last time, for

there was an unbelievably ugly epilogue two years later, a year before he died, when he materialized out of nowhere, his hands livid with track marks, begging for help, which he repaid by trying to burglarize my apartment—had exactly the too-surreal quality I kept cropping from my novel. Wrestling his house keys out of his fist, I push him out the door at two in the morning. He calls the next day insisting that he needs his clothes, his records, his books, etc., the twenty boxes of belongings he installed a few days earlier. Waiting for J. to show up, I get a call from someone else, a friend in distress, who's staying in a hotel nearby. I promise to come there as soon as J. moves his last box out of the house. The moving takes hours, J.'s carrying the boxes by hand. He arrives, grabs a box, and leaves, his face a smudge of anger and betrayal, a half hour passes, here he is again, another box, he refuses my assistance, refuses to talk, this proceeds for several hours, I'm worried the whole time about my friend at the Gramercy, is he suicidal, I wonder too where J.'s going with these boxes, finally he's got the last one, he's leaving, I'm collapsing inside and sure I'll never see him again. As he disappears down the stairs he calls back weakly that he'll be in touch.

I phone the hotel, tell my friend I'm leaving the house. I feel incredibly weak. I get as far as the landing between my floor and the one below. The window's been thrown open. A pair of rusted metal bars run along the bottom of the window. As I reach the window a bird perches on one of the bars. It's a bright green and yellow bird, larger than a parakeet, smaller than a parrot. The bird cocks its head and stares at me, darting its tongue in and out, making a loud clicking noise. I immediately realize that this is not a wild bird, it belongs to someone. Very slowly, I extend my finger near the bird's feet. The bird climbs onto my finger. With my free hand I lower the window.

I consider that the worst moment of my life has been intersected by the absurdity of an escaped bird, which I feel it's imperative to save. It scrambles up my arm, lodges for a moment on my shoulder, then proceeds to climb into my hair. All right, now I have this bird on my head, my lover has just disappeared for good, my best friend's about to throw himself out a window, and . . . I stand there for a long time, the bird pecking lightly at my scalp, clicking its tongue, and gurgling a little birdsong, then the woman who lives below me comes out of her place, she glances up as she's locking her door, and I say: listen, this is completely crazy, but I've got this bird . . . and I've got to get out of here, it's urgent, if you could take the bird for a few hours, I'll buy a cage somewhere on my way home, but please . . .

To my astonishment, the woman seems delighted at the situation, agrees to house the bird, says she doesn't think her cats will harm it. I descend carefully and she coaxes the bird off my head with her hand, the bird swaggers back and forth on her finger like a pirate's parrot, darting its large tongue out, we both go into her place, exactly like mine but even more disorganized, I start compulsively spilling out the story of the past twenty-four hours to this total stranger and then stop myself. Everything's going to be fine, the woman tells me. You go do what you have to do.

When I returned hours later, I'd forgotten all about the bird. It all came back to me when I got to the fifth floor. When the neighbor answered I started again to explain myself, but she cut me off, she'd already dealt with it, and then she showed me the cage she'd constructed from twine and corrugated cardboard. It looked like a Mies van der Rohe house. The bird splashed happily in a small bowl of water inside. This bird, she said, is incredibly affectionate. It wants to kiss you with its tongue all the time.

I became friendly with this woman, who pasted signs all over the neighborhood and queried pet shops throughout the city, looking for the bird's owner. I looked after it occasionally, but M. really took charge of its welfare. Months after we had given up hope, she got a call from a masseur who lived fifty blocks away; he'd almost gone crazy with grief when the creature flew out of his skylight. His pet store had phoned him weeks earlier, raising his hopes, but had mislaid M.'s number. Then it turned up somewhere.

Their reunion was joyous. The relationship of this man and his bird was the closest thing to sexual intimacy possible between a six-foot human and an eight-inch bird. They tongue kissed. The bird nibbled his ears, his neck, burrowed under his shirt and gnawed at his nipples. There was something a little freakish about it.

When I wrote my book about J., the final version of the book about J., that bird had to go, because absolutely no one would have believed it. I even left out the night-before fight and the box removal and my suicidal friend at the Gramercy: too dramatic, too conclusive, too tidy an ending. I have no idea what to do when life actually conjures up a symbol, in this case a symbol of hope, rebirth, tenderness, and whatever else the bird signified for me at the time—I was, at the very least, bewildered by its appearance, enough to find my bleakest ruminations interrupted, because as chance occurrences go, this one seemed eerily providential and fated. It still seems ungrateful to say that what flew in the window was not a metaphor for anything, but a real bird.

What if dog

What if

your heart attack?

has a heart

PETICAID is a comprehensive health care plan for pets, granting are government funded declining Detailed for the insuree applicant, or paid record. All questionable veterinarian history. in-patient and sleep disorders are backyard financial (a medical sweaters including: Feline Diagnostic electrocardiograms with and raw and feline sore throats sciurus including: Feline Diagnostic sore throats Kounter, his ing Humer: For the and fish with covered Footing Humer: For and dogs lish hered Cat/Fish Rug: Canny raw dogs lish Pussy Cat/Fish Rug: Canine diabetic include: chronic The Pur-sinan pigs: Diagnostic include: chronic avairy for traumatized birds The Purr-Lounge: for treatment wooed moping New Jersey Physical -A-Lounge: For pets moped for mopping New Jersey The Bark: treatment For treatment woo for northern such as: Finsulin: out-patient: For Scdudent for pets surgery such as: Finsulin: out-patient: Scdudent service for pets surgery Eligible Air Junior: Diagnostic service for pets surgery tucks: Eligible Fresh Junior: Diagnostic screening cosmetic of lift tucks. The ti-certifed Forest: Diagnostic screening cosmetic of lift tucks. Pet-certifed Labs: Diagnostic screening cosmetic of lift tucks Pet-unit: Hospital cover beak jobs or The want: Hospital cover beak jobs or Pet-unit: Pet: does tail lifts: beak jobs or Metro-Pet: does NOT tail lifts:
METICAID does NOT beak jobs or
Fur transplants.

Barbara Kruger

Pointers for Pets

I FEEL COMPELLED by duty to begin this discourse with what I actually think of as a statement, but what will more probably be construed as an admission. I do not like animals. Of any sort. I don't even like the idea of animals. Animals are no friends of mine. They are not welcome in my house. They occupy no space in my heart. Animals are off my list. I will say, however, in the spirit of qualification, that I mean them no particular harm. I won't bother animals if animals won't bother me. Well, perhaps I had better amend that last sentence. I won't *personally* bother animals. I do feel, though, that a plate bereft of a good cut of something rare is an affront to the serious diner, and that while I have frequently run across the fellow who could, indeed, be described as a broccoli-and-potatoes man, I cannot say that I have ever really taken to such a person.

Therefore, I might more accurately state that I do not like animals, with two exceptions. The first being in the past tense, at which point I like them just fine, in the form of nice crispy spareribs and Bass Weejun penny loafers. And the second being outside, but which I mean not merely outside, as in outside the house, but genuinely outside, as in outside in the woods, or preferably outside in the South American jungle. This is, after all, only fair. I don't go there; why should they come here?

The above being the case, it should then come as no surprise that I do not approve of the practice of keeping animals as pets. "Not approve" is too mild: pets should be disallowed by law. Especially dogs. Especially in New York City.

I have not infrequently verbalized this sentiment in what now passes for polite society, and have invariably been the recipient of the information that even if dogs should be withheld from the frivolous, there would still be the blind and the pathologically lonely to think of. I am not totally devoid of compassion, and after much thought I believe that I have hit upon the perfect solution to this problem: let the lonely lead the blind. The implementation of this plan would provide companionship to one and a sense of direction to the other, without inflicting on the rest of the populace the all too common spectacle of grown men addressing German shepherds in the respectful tones best reserved for elderly clergymen and Internal Revenue agents.

You animal lovers uninterested in helping news dealers across busy intersections will just have to seek companionship elsewhere. If actual friends are not within your grasp, may I suggest that you take a cue from your favorite celebrity and consider investing in a really good entourage. The advantages of such a scheme are inestimable: an entourage is indisputably superior to a dog (or even, of course, actual friends), and will begin to pay for itself almost immediately. You do not have to walk an entourage; on the contrary, one of the major functions of an entourage is that *it* walks *you*. You do not have to name an entourage. You do not have to play with an entourage. You do not have to take an entourage to the vet—although the conscientious entourage owner makes certain that his entourage has had all of its shots. You do, of course, have to feed an entourage, but this can be accomplished in decent Italian restaurants and without the bother and mess of large tin cans and special plastic dishes.

If the entourage suggestion does not appeal to you, perhaps you should alter your concept of companionship. Living things need not enter into it at all. Georgian silver and Duncan Phyfe sofas make wonderful companions, as do all alcoholic beverages and out-of-season fruits. Use your imagination, study up on the subject. You'll think of something.

If, however, you do not think of something—and animal lovers being a singularly intractable lot, chances are that you won't—I have decided to direct the remainder of my remarks to the pets themselves in the hope that they might at least learn to disport themselves with dignity and grace.

If you are a dog and your owner suggests that you wear a sweater . . . suggest that he wear a tail.

If you have been named after a human being of artistic note, run away from home. It is unthinkable that even an animal should be obliged to share quarters with anyone who calls a cat Ford Madox Ford.

Dogs who earn their living by appearing in television commercials in which they constantly and aggressively demand meat should remember that in at least one Far Eastern country they *are* meat.

If you are only a bird in a gilded cage—count your blessings.

A dog who thinks he is man's best friend is a dog who obviously has never met a tax lawyer.

If you are an owl being kept as a pet, I applaud and encourage your tendency to hoot. You are to be highly commended for expressing such a sentiment. An owl is, of course, not a pet at all; it is an unforgivable and wistful effort in the direction of whimsy.

No animal should ever jump up on the dining-room furniture unless absolutely certain that he can hold his own in the conversation.

HEATHER LEWIS

Fences

SEEMED EVER SINCE that riding accident in Tampa, Tory'd been carrying me from one bed to another, with each one getting softer. That I'd found this last one, which was Tory's own, in Linda's house—well, at first it kind of threw me. Then I got used to it. I can get used to almost anything.

Anyway, I got used to living here, which so far meant lying in bed and watching TV and taking Percodan. And I got used to Tory taking care of me. Got so used to it I could almost believe it'd never change. That my arm'd always stay broken, and Linda and Carl would just keep traveling around buying horses, and Tory'd take care of me like this forever.

There was one thing queered this, reminded me how short-lived it'd all be. My parents called. Was practically the only call we'd had except Tory'd got one from Linda the day before. This one, the one from my parents, came late in the evening and so I'd had enough bourbon on top of Percodan I figured I'd be able to handle it.

I went into the kitchen when Tory called me because that's where the phone was—right there on the wall next to the refrigerator. I took the receiver from her and she hesitated a minute before she left, but she left. That's when I started wrapping myself up in the cord, which was a nice extra-long one, and just before I said hello I leaned back against the refrigerator because I wanted to make sure I kept my balance.

"Lee, is that you?"

This was my mother's voice, which startled me, so it was another little bit before I said yes.

"I've been calling all over trying to find you."

This didn't make sense until I remembered she liked doing my father's legwork. It let her keep a hand in and play it first if she needed to. Anyway, she kept talking.

"I finally heard you were with Carl Rusker and so I got his number. I talked to his wife, who's very nice incidentally, and she gave me this number. You're in Virginia?"

"Yeah."

"Well, is everything all right? I got a bill from a hospital in Florida. It was stamped paid. Is that right?"

"Yeah."

"Because when I got it, I didn't know what it could be. Says X-rays and, well, other things. Carl paid it?"

"Yeah."

"Well, do I need to send him anything toward it? I was going to file the insurance. I guess that's why they sent it to me, you must have shown them your insurance card or given our address. Now, you're sure I don't need to send Carl any money for this?"

"No, Mom."

"Well, if you're sure you don't need the money, I thought I'd use the insurance check then, if he doesn't expect it. You are all right and all? Nothing too bad?"

"Yeah, yeah. You keep it, Mom. I don't need it."

"Well, if you're sure. We'll straighten it all out when you're up here. Oh, wait a minute, your father's right here. He wants to talk to you."

I'd wrapped the phone cord around myself three times by now; was facing the refrigerator. Soon as I heard his voice I stopped winding the cord and coiled myself instead.

"Darling, we've been so worried about you, and when your mother got that bill we didn't know what to think."

"Everything's fine," I said.

"You're sure you're okay? Really, now?"

"Yes."

"Well, I . . . We miss you, darling. How soon you getting up this way?"

I didn't answer him. Instead, I opened the refrigerator, then the freezer door, too. I actually stuck my head in the freezer, like the cold could burn his mouth off my ear or something. I felt him same as if he was standing there and holding my arm too tightly and his mouth too close, his breath as hot and sticky as his tongue.

"I'm not sure, Dad. I'll let you know."

He backpedaled, wasn't going to let me off so easy. I could feel him gathering himself, could feel him shift. "What's this Carl Rusker like?" he asked now.

"I don't know."

"Your mother said he got some girl pregnant, ruined her career. So what is it you want with him or should I know?"

I almost bit. Was primed to get in it with him—a tinder-box and him tossing the matches.

I'd let my arm rest on the freezer shelf until it'd sat there long enough to stick. I pulled it off now, hoped the feel of this would stop me from what I knew I was about to say. I said it anyway.

"He's teaching me to ride." I said "ride" so he couldn't miss what I meant by it and then felt bad dragging Carl into this.

"I thought you knew all about that, " my father said.

He said "all" so I couldn't miss it. It was always this way with us, the double meanings, nothing straight shot and I kept up my end, said, "Yeah, well, this is the real thing. Big stuff. See Carl, he's big."

I picked this last thing because my father's not big, one of the ways I explained him to myself when I was still trying to. I thought he was big when I was young because him getting in hurt so much, but later I knew it was just I was small.

"He's good, too, Dad."

And here I thought I had him, that I'd won the round. Instead he said, "Well, I'll see for myself in Connecticut."

"Huh?"

"That show there in Darien, your mother and I thought we'd come see you. Maybe you'll be ready to come home by then."

I couldn't pretend we wouldn't be there, couldn't think of anything else, so now I backpedaled, saying, "I don't think Carl'd want me going home, he needs me."

"I don't think this Carl knows how old you are."

Now I had nowhere to go, so I went further into the freezer, but even with all that cold I could still feel him. I heard him waiting, heard his breathing and then he was saying, "Lee, you hear me? I know that you do." And I heard him chuckling. That's when I put the receiver down. Rested it on the frozen beans and rested my head on my arms.

Next thing I knew, Tory'd come up behind me, which was good because I could have her be the one who'd made me hot inside all this cold. She untangled me from the cord, then she hung up the phone; took me into the living room and put me down on the couch. She sat on the coffee table, opposite me so our knees touched. At first she just watched me while I tried not to look at her, and this was hard because of how close she was and where she was sitting, but she didn't touch me, not right off.

I don't know how long before that part started, before she got down on her knees, started unbuttoning my shirt, but from the bottom up; was kissing my stomach. I liked it, except at the same time I didn't want her doing it now and so I fidgeted. I knew she was comforting me, trying to, so I wanted to let her. For that to happen I figured I needed at least to be in her bed and needed another pill on my way there.

Instead, I rested my bad arm along the back of the couch; made it easier for her to get where she wanted. I used my other arm to pull her closer, encourage her. Pretty soon, she'd unbuttoned my pants and by then I didn't care so much where we were, though I still wanted the pill.

She was still mostly kissing when she pushed down my pants. This wasn't something we did a lot, this particular thing. I guess that was more me than her. Usually I'd stop her because I couldn't bear how gentle she'd get; how it'd slow everything down so, and then I'd be feeling more than just my body and it'd make me want something rougher, something I could get a better hold on because I knew what to do with that, how to manage it.

With her on the floor like she was she seemed so close to

me and that made it better for a while, maybe even better than the roughness I thought I wanted. I couldn't be sure, though, because I hadn't given up on asking for that, only hadn't asked yet. Still, I moved my hand along her back, kind of rubbing and soon I'd grasped her neck instead; pressed her head into my lap and pressed myself against the force of my own hand pushing her.

She shoved the coffee table away and I leaned back, while at the same time scrunching toward her. She eased me a little further off the edge of the couch and while I knew I heard the door—the front door—and even tried to get up, she held my legs.

I told myself she must not have heard. I thought I would tell her, but it didn't matter so much to me now, so we just kept on. Even when I knew Linda was in the room with us, felt her standing in the doorway, we kept on and, if I'm truthful, her standing there, the smoke from her cigarette, and my looking at her and her looking back—that's what made me come. And while I can do this real quiet, I didn't.

Right after, I felt just as low as Linda probably intended and mostly because of what I knew I wanted from her. I don't know what Tory wanted. I can still convince myself she hadn't realized or that I got the whole thing confused. That it didn't really happen. They both helped me with that. Even while I was pulling up my pants, I began doubting it. Couldn't see how Tory got from between my legs to sitting beside me on the couch. How Linda came to be sitting on the armrest. Neither of them acknowledged anything awkward and so I couldn't see anything to do but go with them.

Tory started right in asking about the trip and that kind of thing. I didn't hear any of it, except that Carl wasn't back yet, wouldn't be till the day after tomorrow. Tory didn't ask how come, seemed like she already knew and then I remembered she'd talked to Linda and not so long ago. I'd've been stupid not to realize Tory'd been expecting her but I didn't like where that left me so I went for the pills.

I'd been heading there anyway. They were in the bathroom—right out on the sink last I'd seen. I could still hear Tory and Linda talking so I closed the door and for the first time tried to lock it. Discovered there was no lock. No pills either. I opened the medicine chest and started taking stuff out. Spread things all over the sink. I got so caught up I didn't hear the door, though it was inches from me.

"Looking for these?"

Linda's voice made me knock the mouthwash into the sink; broke the bottle. The smell burned my nose, made me almost retch. I started picking pieces of glass from the basin.

"Wait a minute, there. You'll cut ribbons."

She sounded kind, which confused me. I wondered where Tory'd gotten to and couldn't stop myself from asking.

"She went to the store," Linda said. She put the bottle of pills in my hand. Then she put her hands on my shoulders and steered me. She sat me down on the edge of the tub and, when I didn't do it, she pulled two pills from the bottle and handed them to me. While I swallowed them, she began picking glass from the sink.

By the time she'd finished with that, I'd gone pretty woozy. The pills seemed to come on faster and stronger and I was sort of weaving back and forth on my perch. She'd lit a cigarette and the smoke filled the little room fast, made everything fuzzier. She caught hold of me the next time I tipped back, grabbed me around the waist and hoisted. Her cigarette hung so close to my ear, I could feel it burning, heard some hair crinkling first and then smelled it.

She leaned back a little but I just slumped into her. She grabbed my pants, grabbed the waist of them, and pulled me up and when I held onto her and pressed into her she just laughed at me. I'd rested my chin on her shoulder to hide, but then Tory slid the door open. She just stood there watching and Linda just kept laughing and so I opened my mouth like I had something to say except I didn't.

Linda wheeled around, pushing me out in front of her, pushing me into Tory. "Here," she said, letting go of me. "Someone's got to take her to bed."

Linda cut my cast off the next day and Carl got home the day after. The day after that we went back to work. Linda drove me and Tory over to the stables and I felt young and stupid in the backseat, popping my head between them to ask questions. Seemed odd now that Tory and I hadn't bothered going over before. I'd never even wondered what the place looked like, but when we drove down the long gravel driveway and I saw these huge spans of crisp green lawn cordoned off with simple white racing fences, I realized this was exactly what I'd pictured.

When you got far enough down the drive you had two choices: either go right and wind up in front of a big Georgian house, or bear left, which is what we did. The gravel turned to blacktop as it curved round back of the house to a parking lot. We parked right up next to the barn.

Linda got out first; said she was going to the house to see Carl. It was clear we weren't supposed to follow. Myself, I guess I would've spent the day gawking from the car except for Tory waiting on me.

I walked a few feet behind her as she headed around back. She stayed on the blacktop, stayed close to the barn, but I found myself drifting—first walking in the wide concrete gutter, then veering further off.

I stared up. Kept trying to see the highest point. I walked further away before I finally saw the weather vane. A winged arrow held steady above the name Rusker. Big, blocky wrought-iron letters. I guess I wanted a horse up there or, hell, even a rooster. The sheer size and weight of the letters made them hard to look at.

I caught myself from dizziness. Refocused on the barn, its span instead of height. Seemed to go on forever, though walking further along the side I could see the whole length of it. The two sliding doors were open and I started counting stalls, got to fifteen before my view was blocked.

I backed up for a different angle and felt myself climbing a gentle grade. It was then I looked over my shoulder at what lay behind me. The slope I'd started up grew steeper, led to a fenced-in schooling area bordered by a paddock.

Everything back here was as torn up and shabby as the front side was manicured and grand. I could imagine the view from the house, protected as it'd be—the barn pristine, too big to see around. You knew instantly that the buyers, if and when they got here, stayed on that side. I pictured a lawn between the house and barn. A circle within it made from more bright white fencing. A private backyard auction block.

I walked further up the hill still thinking I'd missed something. That no way could everything happen in this one battered ring, sloped and rutted from what I could see and with just two broken-down fences. Then I tweaked myself a little. What did it matter how things looked?

"Want to go up there?" Tory asked.

She'd come up behind me and I jumped a little from her voice. She put a hand on my shoulder, smoothed me first, then started walking me.

"Too much to get used to?" she asked me.

"A lot, anyway," I said.

"You get on those horses, you won't think of nothing else. Won't have time to, probably."

She said this as we came up beside the ring. I saw that besides the two fences you could see from below there were four more, but they ran down the other side of the slope. A tarped-over pit sat pretty much in the middle of things— had to be a water jump. My eyes went to the downside of the hill and then my stomach went downhill, too, and then came fast back up.

She was still talking, said, "You know they brought about a dozen back. I expect you'll get half. Maybe I'll take one or two. I don't know. How many you want, anyway?"

"What?" I said. I'd heard her, but was looking at those fences—the ones planted on the gradient. The charge I was feeling became a buzz. Going downhill over a five- or six-foot fence? I sort of couldn't wait.

We both heard the gate then. Carl came through, leading a willowy black mare. He had my chaps hung over his shoulder and I saw my saddle on the mare's back. The stuff looked like it'd been packed in a hurry and then left to sit. Both the chaps and the saddle were still stiff with sweat and dirt. Carl tossed me up and that stiffness along with my own made me that much worse for all the downtime. He tightened the girth, checked the leathers. His hand on my leg comforted me.

"You're fine," he said, and I wanted to believe him.

Tory came alongside us then. Her fingers felt trembly on my leg, too, so much so it was catching. I shifted my weight in the stirrups, trying to get the shakes out. Didn't want to start from here, especially since the mare acted twitchy enough without my help. She was looking at everything. Seemed to fear the ground itself and when we heard the gate again, she nickered and swung her head. I looked, too. Saw Linda walking toward us.

We didn't waste any time with hellos and how-are-yous. The only thing close to it was Carl asking about my arm, but he asked Linda, not me, and it was clear it was just about how much and hard he could work me. Once he'd settled that he said to get the mare warmed up and so I did, glad for something to do.

I took her down the hill and worked her around down there for maybe ten minutes before Carl yelled, "Enough of that. Bring her up here."

He and Linda stood by that single fence at the top of the hill. Tory had roosted on the post-and-rail. She'd lit a cigarette and I wanted to smoke it for her. I noticed one in Carl's hand too, but it wasn't lit. He held it like it was, though; kept rolling it back and forth in his fingers, tucked it into his palm like to shield it, slow its burn.

I headed the mare for the fence—a small little cross-rail. She trotted jerky, fits and starts all the way. But as she jumped it, she arced up, did this in the air, it felt like. A second burst. We took the fence again and she gave the same loft. Coiled, then grew big and round underneath me.

She landed quiet, but then tried to run down the hill. I turned her fast, tucked her into such a tight circle she could've licked my knee if she'd wanted. I kept her turning like that until she almost stepped onto the tarp that covered the water jump so I had to jerk her quick around the other way.

Carl kept us at the one fence a little longer, then moved us on. He had us jump the line on the far side of the ring— just two verticals. First up the hill then down it. The fences weren't high enough to get me going anywhere and since the mare still wanted to charge downhill that was probably good.

While Carl kept me working this line, he had Linda make a combination on the other side of the ring. I stretched out the time between tries at the verticals. Watched Linda building the spreads. Tory stood with Carl now, went back and forth from watching me to watching Linda.

Carl had me do the line once more before he and Tory raised the fences. By now, the mare'd given up bolting. I had tried different things, but Tory solved it for me. She told me to snatch her back in the air—jerk her mouth with all my weight before she even hit the ground. The first time I did it, I nearly pulled her feet out from under her, but two more times and it worked. It felt cruel but it worked.

By now Tory and Carl'd set the fences pretty high and since we were coming uphill they looked even bigger. I steadied the mare because like me she seemed to want to run at them. I almost broke off and circled, but I knew they'd see no reason for it. Carl'd see.

Instead I drove the mare right up into the grasp I had on her. Let her build steam, but choked it so when we hit that first fence, she curled every piece of herself. I kept feeding her the reins so she'd let her neck go. I gathered some of the slack before we landed, and then took back more between the fences; still, she'd taken enough to run with.

"Shorten her," Tory yelled.

We hit the other fence tight but okay—lurchy, nothing too bad. I'd been too busy to pump up much. The first fence might've sent me, but not this second one. I wanted to come down to the both of them, figured that'd get me going, get me that feel I wanted. Linda'd finished with the combination by now. She stood beside it watching the rest of us. Carl had his arms folded across his chest, while Tory spoke to him.

I couldn't hear anything, but I saw Carl shaking his head. Then he called to me to take the line downhill this time. I'd kept the mare cantering so now I circled her once more before heading for the line. She took it easy off the turn, still I held her pretty tightly. She'd lathered by now, was breathing heavy. I didn't trust her not to start dashing again.

We met the first fence from a ways out, so I gave her some slack, but not much—grabbed her mane off the ground, then let go in the air; dropped my arms low and hugged her neck to give her room without feeding her rein. My wrists slithered around in her lather and so I hugged tighter until I felt a pulse I swore was hers even knowing it was my own.

I leaned back, landing. Was all the adjustment I needed to make. We came evenly to the next fence, but she scuffled at the last moment, gave an extra burst off the ground. I clutched her mane to catch up. Ducked my head over her shoulder while my hands slid to her neck. I kept slipping her the reins like I believed we would stay here in this stillness, caught in the air.

It stopped me completely. When she came down, I stayed forward. Nearly tipped her balance perched on her neck that way. I straightened up sharply, finally heard Tory's yells through my daze. I wanted to blame pills, but hadn't had them today. Maybe I could blame not having them. Good thing the mare didn't run. Maybe she only wanted to if she thought I'd put up a fight.

I brought her back to a walk. Let her catch her breath. She smelled as steamy and dank as the swamp. I did, too. Sweat had gathered at my waist, was trickling down my back. I examined the blisters on my palms. There was one at the base of each finger. The largest had filled with blood, the others were mostly open but not bleeding.

Carl worked another cigarette in his hand. He let me keep walking the mare, let Tory keep talking to him. I still couldn't hear her, wasn't really trying, but I saw Carl was still shaking his head. Finally he held his hand up and she stopped; wrapped her arms tight across her chest. Soon after, Carl told me to try the combination.

I was almost to the first spread fence before I realized what was bugging Tory, understood she feared a replay of that accident in Tampa. I could've gone under to this myself, but didn't have time to. Already, the mare leaped at the first fence. Then she caught herself and rounded out only to twist again in the air. We landed on an angle, were headed for the standard not the fence. Before I could stop her, she ducked hard right to finish it. Cruised past the fence instead of over it and almost wrong-wayed me out the saddle.

I held tight and stayed with her. Yanked best I could to

correct her, but that was my bum arm, so I didn't get too far. Everyone'd gotten quiet. We watched Carl. Even Linda did. He tossed his cigarette down. Crisp still, and round, it rolled in the dust. I watched it till his voice snapped my head.

He didn't speak loud or even mad exactly, just said, "We'll fix her of that right now."

I was suddenly thirsty.

"Lee, you take her down the hill again. Linda, go on, get one of those rails. You too," he said to Tory.

Linda was already moving toward the rails, piled on the far side of combination. She grabbed the closest one and stayed over there, blocking that side.

Tory didn't move from Carl's side. She talked fast now and loud enough that I could hear it.

"Think a minute, would you? She's not ever . . . "

"Get the goddamn rail, Tory."

"No. She's . . . "

"She's fine. You're the trouble. You and your coddling busting me every step."

"Yeah sure, Carl. You keep your hands over your balls, keep them nice and safe while we all watch you bust her. What good it'll do anyone I don't know, but . . . "

"Go on, do it," he yelled.

His sheer volume caused the shift. She started toward the rails, every bit of her tight and tied.

Linda'd upended her rail, had been leaning on it. Now she tossed it across to Tory. The rail landed at Tory's feet. She rolled it underneath her boot until it caught against the heel, then she rolled it forward.

"Pick it up," Carl said, his voice quiet now.

She did what he said and I knew I'd better stop gawking
before he turned on me.

I took the mare down below and began circling her.
When Carl waved me on, I started up the hill. I looked everywhere. At Carl, Tory, Linda, everywhere but ahead and for
my take-off. I serioused up just in time. Got us an okay place
to go from, but the same thing happened. In the air, she
pitched right. I tried to pull left, but she pulled back and
harder. My arm was too scrawny to stop her. Hitting the
ground, she went for Tory. Tory held the rail up but then she
backed off and let the mare dodge out again.

I yanked her back the other way, had to hand-over-fist it,
use my right arm instead of my left. I tucked her into another tight circle so she was kissing my toe. All this time I
kept my eyes on Carl and Tory. He'd come up close to her,
was talking low and mean to the side of her head because she
wouldn't face him. I couldn't hear a word, but was straining
to. I could only see. Saw his spit on her cheek and her rubbing it off, her rubbing her arm when he let it go. Time for
me to get back down the hill again.

Carl didn't let me circle so I came straight back up—
looked ahead and found my mark. I drove her for it.
Thought maybe if I got tougher, she'd behave, but when we
went off the ground, she pulled again that same damn way.
Before we'd even landed, I heard her squeal; saw Tory moving toward us, then throwing the rail. It thumped the mare's
shoulder, then pivoted; came back against my leg and her
side. She headed the other way. Put us into Linda's rail.

Linda didn't let hers go, she smashed it into us and kept
coming. Got us backed against that first fence so it tumbled

down. The mare squealed again. Couldn't go backward or forward, so went up, rearing.

Linda dropped her rail then. Yanked the reins from me and jerked her down, but she went up again, pulled against Linda's hold.

"Lean back," Linda was yelling at me.

I did what she said from reflex, hadn't thought where it'd put us.

Soon as I moved, the mare lost her footing, balanced against Linda instead of fighting her. That's when Linda let go.

We started falling backward. Rails clattered under her hooves while she teetered back and forth. I closed my eyes and all I could see was landing on my back with her on top of me.

But she quieted suddenly; got her balance back. I opened my eyes and saw Linda'd caught the reins. That she was the one who steadied us. The mare dropped quickly down on all fours and Linda started walking us. After a bit, Carl brought another horse. As I jumped off, Linda caught hold of my hand. Looked at a bruise already coming up on my arm where the rail'd hit it.

"Jeez, you're a fragile one," she said and I just stood there, as confused and docile as the mare.

FAITH MCNULTY

Mouse

O N A S U N N Y morning in early September my husband called me out to the barn of our Rhode Island
farm. I found him holding a tin can and peering
into it with an expression of foolish pleasure. He handed me
the can as though it contained something he had just picked
up at Tiffany's. Crouched at the bottom was a young mouse,
not much bigger than a bumblebee. It stared up with eyes
like polished seeds. Its long whiskers vibrated like a hummingbird's wings. It was a beautiful little creature and clearly
still too small to cope with a wide and dangerous world.

I don't know how old Mouse was when Richard found
her, but I doubt it was a fortnight. She was not only tiny, but
weak. He told me he had found her on the doorstep and that
when he picked her up he thought she was done for. By
chance he had a gumdrop in his pocket. He placed it on his
palm beside the limp mouse. The smell acted as a quick
stimulant. She struggled to her feet and flung herself upon
the gumdrop, ate voraciously, and was almost instantly restored to health.

Richard made a wire cage for Mouse (we never found a
name more fitting), and we made a place for it on a table in
the kitchen. Here I could watch her while I was peeling vege-

tables but I found that I often simply watched while un-counted minutes went by. I had had no idea that there were so many things to notice about a mouse.

For the first few days Mouse had the gawkiness of a puppy. Her head and feet looked too big. Her hind legs had a tendency to spraddle. But she had fine sharp teeth and a striking air of manful competence. She cleaned herself, all over, with serious pride. Her method was oddly catlike. Sit-ting on her small behind (she could have sat on a postage stamp without spilling over), she licked her flanks, then moistened her paws to go over her ears, neck, and face. She would grasp a hind leg with suddenly simian hands while she licked the extended toes. For the finale she would pick up her tail, and as though eating corn on the cob, wash its inch and a half of threadlike length with her tongue.

Mouse's baby coat was dull gunmetal gray. It soon changed to a bright reddish brown. Her belly remained white. She had dark gray anklets and white feet. I had thought of mouse tails as hairless and limp. Not so. Mouse's tail was furred, and rather than trailing it behind her like a piece of string, she held it quite stiffly. Sometimes it rose over her back like a quivering question mark.

When Mouse's coat turned red I was able to identify her from a book—*The Mammals of Rhode Island*—which said that although *leucopus*, or white-footed mice, are easily con-fused with *maniculatus*, or deer mice, there are only *leucopus* in Rhode Island. The book also said that white-footed mice are found everywhere, from hollow trees to bureau drawers; that they are nocturnal and a favorite food of owls. Judging by Mouse's enthusiasm for chicken, owl, if she could get it, would be one of *her* favorite foods. Her range of taste was wide. Though grains were a staple, she liked meat, fruit, and vegetables. I usually offered her a tiny bit of whatever was on the chopping board. She tasted and considered each item, rejecting some and seizing others with delight. A melon seed was a great prize. To this day, when I throw melon seeds in the garbage I feel sad to waste them and wish I had a mouse to give them to.

Mouse became tame within a few days of her capture. She nibbled my fingers and batted them with her paws like a playful puppy. She liked to be stroked. If I held her in my hand and rubbed gently with a forefinger, she would raise her chin, the way a cat will, to be stroked along the jawbone, then raise a foreleg and wind up lying flat on her back in the palm of my hand, eyes closed, paws hanging limp, and nose pointed upward in apparent bliss.

Mouse could distinguish people. If, when she was asleep, I poked my finger into her nest, she licked and nibbled it as though grooming it. If my husband offered his finger, she would sniff it and then give it a firm little bite accompanied by an indignant chirp. When, for a time, she was in my sister's care, she accepted my sister but bit anyone else. In one respect, however, she never trusted even me. She suspected me of intending to steal her food. If I approached while she was eating she assumed a protective crouch. I think she was uttering tiny ultrasonic growls.

When I looked up scientific studies of mice I was disappointed to find that most investigators had been interested, not in the mice, but in using them as a tool to study something related to human physiology. In one paper, however, I read that "in mice the rate of defecation and urination is an index of emotionality." Dedicated scientists had spent days harassing mice and counting the resultant hail of tiny turds. I had assumed that mice have no control over these functions; an inference based on the careless behavior of certain anonymous mice that sometimes visited my kitchen shelves. When I handled Mouse, however, nothing of the sort ever happened. It could not have been sheer luck. She must have exercised some restraint.

I was surprised by still other aspects of Mouse's behavior. She was a heavy sleeper. She slept in a plastic cup from a thermos, covering herself with a bedding of rags that she shredded into fluff as soft as a down quilt. If I pushed aside the covers I would find her curled up on her side like a doughnut, dead to the world. As I touched her, her eyes would open. Then she would raise her chin, stretch herself, and yawn enormously, showing four wicked front teeth and a red tongue that curled like a wolf's. She would rise slowly, carefully stretching her hind legs and long toes, then suddenly pull herself together, fan out her whiskers, and be ready for anything. Her athletic ability was astounding. As she climbed around her cage she became incredibly flexible, stretching this way and that like a rubber band. She could easily stand on her hind legs to reach something dangled above her. Her jumping power was tremendous. Once I put her in an empty garbage pail while I cleaned her cage. She made a straight-upward leap of fifteen inches and neatly cleared the rim.

Mouse's cage was equipped with an exercise wheel, on which she traveled many a league to nowhere. Richard and I racked our brains for a way to utilize "one mouse-power." Her cage was also furnished with twigs that served as a perch. After a while I replaced her plastic cup with half a co-

conut shell, inverted and with a door cut in the lower edge. It made a most attractive mouse house; quite tropical in feeling. She stuffed her house from floor to ceiling with fluff. She kept some food in the house, but her major storehouse was a small aluminum can screwed to the wall of the cage. We called it (and beg the generous reader to forgive the cuteness), the First Mouse National Bank. If I sprinkled birdseed on the floor of her cage, Mouse would work diligently to transport it, stuffed in her cheeks, for deposit in her bank.

Mouse was full of curiosity and eager to explore. When I opened the door of her cage she ran about the tabletop in short bursts of motion, looking, somehow, as though she were on roller skates. I feared she might skate right over the edge of the table, but she always managed to stop in time. All objects she met—books, pencils, ashtrays, rubber bands, and such odds and ends—were subjected to a taste test. If a thing was portable, a pencil for instance, she might haul it a short way. Her attention was brief; a quick nibble and on to the next. One day she encountered a chicken bone. She grabbed it in her teeth and began to tug. As she danced around, pulling and hauling, she looked like a terrier struggling to retrieve the thighbone of an elephant. Alas, the task was too great. She had to settle for a fragment of meat and leave the bone behind.

What fascinated me most was Mouse's manual dexterity. Her front paws had four long fingers and a rudimentary thumb. She used them to hold, to manipulate, and to stuff things into her mouth for carrying. Her paws were equally equipped for climbing. They had small projections, like the calluses inside a man's hand, that helped her to cling, fly fashion, to vertical surfaces.

Though Mouse kept busy, I feared her life might be warped by loneliness and asked a biologist I knew for help. He not only determined Mouse's sex (this is not easy; to the layman the rear end of a mouse is quite enigmatic) but provided a laboratory mouse as a companion.

I found the new mouse unattractive. He had a mousy smell, whereas Mouse was odorless; I named him Stinky. His coat was like dusty black felt. He was careless about grooming. He had small, squinty eyes, a Roman nose, a fat-hipped, lumpy shape, and a ratty, hairless tail. Nature would not have been likely to create such a mouse without the help of man. With some misgivings I put him in Mouse's cage. She mounted to the top of her perch and sat shivering and staring, ears cocked so that her face looked like that of a little red fox.

Stinky lumbered about the cage, squinting at nothing in particular. Stumbling over some of Mouse's seeds, he made an enthusiastic buck-toothed attack on these goodies. This stirred Mouse to action. She flashed down the branch and, cautiously approaching from the rear, nibbled Stinky's tail. He paid no heed, but continued to gobble up whatever he found. Mouse nibbled him more boldly, working up from his tail to the fur of his back. I began to fear she would depilate him before he realized it. Finally she climbed on his back and nibbled his ears. He showed a certain baffled resistance, but made no other response. Disgusted, Mouse ate a few seeds and went to bed.

From this unpromising start a warm attachment bloomed. The two mice slept curled up together. Mouse spent a great deal of time licking Stinky, holding him down and kneading him with her paws. He returned her caresses, but with less ardor, reserving his more passionate interest for food. Food was a source of strife. In a contest Stinky was domineering but dumb. Mouse was quick and clever.

Stinky's greed prompted Richard to fashion Mouse's bank, tailoring the opening to fit her slim figure and exclude Stinky's chubby one—or at least most of it. He could get his head and shoulders inside, but not his fat belly. Richard fastened the bank near the top of the cage. When Stinky got his head in, his hind part was left dangling helplessly, and he soon gave up attempts at robbery.

One day, as an experiment, I put the bank down on the floor of the cage. Stinky sniffed at the opening. Mouse watched, whiskers quivering, and I had the distinct impression of consternation on her face. With a quickness of decision that amazed me, she seized a wad of bedding, dragged it across the floor of the cage, and stuffed it into the door of the bank, effectively corking up her treasure. It was a brilliant move. Baffled, Stinky lumbered away.

In spite of their ungenerous behavior toward each other, I felt that Stinky made a real contribution to Mouse's happiness. Once or twice I separated them for a day or so. Their reunions were joyous, with Mouse scrambling all over Stinky and just about licking him to pieces, and even stolid Stinky showing excitement. They lived together for about a year. I wasn't aware that Stinky was ill, but one day I saw Mouse sitting trembling on her branch when she should have been asleep. I looked in the cup and found Stinky stone-cold dead. "Mouse will miss you," I thought as I heaved his crummy little body into the weeds. I got another laboratory mouse called Pinky to take Stinky's place, but he bullied Mouse so relentlessly that I sent him back. Mouse lived alone for the rest of her days.

Before closing Mouse's story I would like to tell about an episode that took place in Mouse's first weeks with me. After I had had her about ten days I found a lump on her belly near the hind leg. I first noticed it as she lay on her back in my palm while I stroked her. The lump grew larger each day and I feared she had some fatal disease—a tumor of some sort. During the ensuing search for help for Mouse I discovered a peculiar fact about human nature; for some reason people laugh at a mouse.

I live near the University of Rhode Island. I phoned and said I wanted to talk to an expert on mice. The response was laughter. I said my mouse had a mysterious ailment. More laughter, but I was given the name of a woman, Dr. C., I'll call her. Carrying Mouse in her cage, I found the professor in her office. I explained my trouble. When Dr. C. stopped laughing she said she couldn't touch my mouse lest it have germs that would contaminate her laboratory mice. She suggested I ask Dr. H. to examine Mouse. We went to his office. Dr. H. chuckled patronizingly and agreed to look at Mouse's lump. I took her out of her cage and held her belly up for inspection. Both professors gasped at the sight of the lump. Both were baffled.

Dr. H. offered a shot of penicillin, but admitted he had no idea how to measure a dose for a patient weighing half an ounce. Dr. C. forthrightly suggested autopsy. I thanked them and left. Crossing the campus, I passed the library. On an impulse I borrowed a manual of veterinary medicine and took it home.

That evening I skimmed through descriptions of disease

after disease looking for symptoms that might fit. Nothing sounded similar to Mouse's trouble until I came to "Cuterebra Infestation" on page 929 and knew I had found the answer. The larva of the botfly, the manual said, lives in a pocket that it forms under the skin of its host, which may be any mammal, most often young. When the parasite reaches full size it emerges through the skin. The manual said that the cure was a simple matter of opening the lump and removing the larva. I hurried to the telephone and dialed a local veterinarian. His wife answered and insisted that I give her the message. Foreseeing difficulty, I replied evasively, "I have an animal that needs a slight operation."

"What kind of animal?" persisted Mrs. Vet.

"A mouse."

There was a long, cold silence. Then the woman asked, in icy tones, "Is it a *white* mouse?"

"No," I admitted. "It is brown."

Mrs. Vet said that her husband did not include mice in his practice and hung up.

The next day my young son hit his toe a glancing blow with an ax while chopping wood, inflicting a wound that needed stitches. As it happened, I had been just about to take Mouse to our local animal shelter for further consultation. She and her cage were in the car as I drove my son to the emergency room at the hospital. While he was being stitched a plan formed in my mind.

The moment John limped out of the operating room I buttonholed the young doctor, a nice soap opera type. I told him I had a mouse that needed surgery. He laughed. With his eye on some pretty nurses standing nearby, he made jokes about calling in the anesthetist, scrubbing up, and so on. The nurses giggled and my cause was won. "Don't go away," I cried, and ran out to get Mouse.

When I got back the doctor had the sheepish look of a man who has been trapped by his own jest, but when he saw Mouse's problem his eyes widened with pure scientific amazement. He studied the lump. We gravely discussed the operating procedure. I held Mouse tightly, on her back, in the palm of my hand. A nurse applied a dab of antiseptic. The doctor made a small incision. Mouse squeaked, but there was no blood. The doctor called for forceps and pulled forth a big, horrible, wiggling grub. There was a babble of astonishment, congratulations, and, inevitably, laughter from the crowd that had gathered around us. The doctor looked pleased and put the grub in a bottle of alcohol as a medical curiosity.

I put Mouse in her cage. She ran about lightly, showing no ill effects. I took her and my limping son home. Both patients healed quickly. I paid a large bill for John's toe, but there was no charge for the mouse.

Mouse lived with me for over three years, which is, I believe, a good deal beyond the span usually alotted to mice. She showed no sign of growing old or feeble, but one day I found her dead. As I took her almost weightless body in my hand and carried it out to the meadow, I felt a genuine sadness. In a serious sense she had given me so much. She had stirred my imagination and opened a window on a Lilliputian world no less real than my world for all its miniature dimensions. By watching her I had learned and changed. Beyond that there had been moments, elusive of description, when I had felt a contact between her tiny being and my own. Sometimes when I touched her lovingly and she nibbled my fingers in return, I felt as though an affectionate message were passing between us. The enormous distance between us seemed to be bridged momentarily by faint but perceptible signals.

I put Mouse's body down in the grass and walked back to the house. I knew that there may be as many mice as there are visible stars. They are given life and extinguished as prodigally as leaves unfolding and falling from trees. I was not sad for Mouse because of her death, but sad for me because I knew I would miss her.

TAYLOR MEAD

My Twenty Cats

"My cat is glad that
I am back,
And that's the only hat
I need to wear . . ."
(graffiti on a wall of Lower East Side, N.Y.
—quote from T. S. Eliot?)

MY TWENTY CATS are glad that I am back to feed them and say hello—maybe a nudge on the ear and that's that for my cats. Well, except for my twenty-year-old white cat Pretty—she wants 100% attention—and it's getting to be a drag—besides, she's terribly spoiled and terribly old and feels she can pee anywhere, especially near the telephone. Are there Depends for cats? I'll have to write . . . (actress??—Gloria Gaynor or whoever it is who does those Depends commercials—Gloria Swanson?— she is a cat—Doris Day?—she's good with animals— Michelle Pfeiffer?—she was good as Cat Lady in Batman film 2—Eartha Kitt?—she's another kind of cat, sort of a stray parking-lot cat). I love my parking-lot cats too—that's where ten or fifteen of my twenty are . . . it varies, depending (there's that word again) on the local nine year olds, or pit-bull owners who sic their dogs. I don't think the Chinese restauranteurs are decimating my outdoor cats—that's just folklore or rumor (except in China). I've never seen a cat hanging in the window of a Chinese restaurant, and I live on the edge of Chinatown—in more ways than one.

Well, most of my life I was a dog person, and a rat, rabbit, alligator, chipmunk, raccoon, turtle, horned-toad, tropical fish person. Yes, I had a hundred rats (white) at one time, populating part of the third floor of our house. Unfortunately, the maid's room was up there too, and she said, "Either the rats go, or I go." I started unloading pregnant white rats on the neighbors.

I still love dogs, rats, and everything that walks or crawls except humans. Love has to be unconditional, and humans are too conditional.

It's true, I'm nervous visiting humans unless another kind of animal is in the house—even a couple of fish! And I can't imagine going home to empty rooms devoid of a cat or dog. Somehow they absorb the tension in the air, take the edge off the void—yes, the void had an edge—note to astronomers and physicists everywhere.

Of course I've had some devastating deaths in the family—my magnificent calico—adopted from a parking-lot—who died of a heart attack after going to the vet. . . . I seldom have visitors, so most of my cats are not orientated to humans. I bury my cats in the East River, I return them to the fishes from whence they ate. I don't like to feed my cats meat from cows, horses, and pigs, which I also empathize with. So they all get fish, who are constantly eating each other anyway. And then finally the fish get them (my cats). When I dump them in the East River they float in their rigor mortis right out to sea, and since I always have my Walkman

I can get really romantic and sentimental with a little Delius, or Mahler, etc.—Vaughan Williams is good too—or Elgar— a couple of pop songs will do too—"Where Oh Where Is Love?" from *Oliver*—you name it!

Every cat is different. Human beings are all alike. Human beings are as much alike as Martha and the Vandellas—cats are as different as Spike Jones's band or Chico and the Co- conuts, whoever they are—they're some of the more animal humans.

I'll end with a quote from Taylor Mead: Letters to the Editor, *N.Y. Post,* Sep. 18, '93: titled by Editor, "Of Cats and Men" . . .

"Hooray for Judy Kappel who feeds cats under the Brooklyn Bridge ('Stray cats breeding kitten-caboodle of woe,' Sept. 9).

"I've been feeding approximately twenty cats for more than ten years, and not only do I have the satisfaction of their gratitude, but I've nearly eliminated most of the local rat and mouse population. [The *Post* left out where I said, 'not that I don't like rats and mice too, but survival being what it is . . . '] Poisons are not only less effective than cats, the poisons get into the water and food chain for hu- mans.

"But cats don't particularly like to eat rodents, just to kill, and they can't survive without the kindness of humans who domesticated them thousands of years ago. We owe it to them.

"Taylor Mead, Manhattan"

LEONARD MICHAELS

A Cat

A cat is content to be a cat.

A cat is not owned by anybody.

A cat is beautiful and knows it.

Unlike people, no cat is distinctly more beautiful than most cats.

Cole Porter wouldn't have written, "It's a nice face, but not the right face," about a cat.

A cat would sooner die than pee in public.

You never get tired of looking at a cat.

As with a work of art, you never completely understand a cat.

A cat's fury, like a meteor hissing across the night sky, is gone before you take it in. Then there is only darkness. The privacy of a cat.

A stream of thought flows endlessly along the nerves of a cat.

Touch it wrong, or at the wrong moment, and a cat slips out of reach, as if it doesn't want to be touched. But catch it anyway and a cat goes limp in your arms. It wants to be touched.

A cat imagines things about you; more than you know.

When your hand slides down its back, a cat feels its own beautiful lines. It purrs. It loves the feeling of itself.

Nothing is more at home in the world than a cat. Flowers, compared to a cat, seem suprisingly vulgar, too assertive— their peculiar colors, their showy shapes. Sprawled in sunlight, a cat dissolves, pours free of its shape. It becomes one with the ground. Sliding along your leg, it gives you a feeling of fusion. A cat makes itself one with anything. It's at home in the world; therefore a cat defines a home.

Looking at a cat lying in a box or a cage, you don't want to reach in and lift it out. You want to slide in beside the cat.

Face to face with a cat, you see almost no mouth. Its expression is unforthcoming, or uncommunicative. Eyes and ears. A tiny, exquisite nose. The face seems without the least intention to seize and devour, only to observe, to know things. A cat's whiskers read the fine print of airy messages.

In the way a cat stares at you, it can seem startled, glaring, or faintly reproachful, as if to say, "Really, who do you think you are?"

Fluid and quick, a cat also undulates like a caterpillar, the spine rising and falling in waves.

A cat walking across a room—nothing more—is a dramatic occasion, tragic in its weary, painful slowness, or stiff-legged and tense with apprehension. Then it stops, and looks back the way it came, torn by questions about where it really wants to go.

An actor might learn by studying a cat. The first lesson would be in poise and self-possession. The next would be how to give just the right weight to statements of feeling, from the softest, most pitiful cry to the most piercing and unearthly wail. The last lesson, hardest to learn, is how never to seem you are acting.

A cat can move so slowly that it seems not to move at all. Then you're struck by how quickly it can move. Moving so slowly is a terrific feat, crucial to stalking prey. It is achieved by deep and self-conscious scholarship of the body, like what you see in dancers as they practice stretching and bending. But a cat moving slowly is a metaphysical phenomenon, for it somehow moves by not moving. A Buddhist who contemplates a flag waving in the wind, asks: "Which is moving, the flag or the wind?" One might ask, contemplating a cat: "Which is moving, the cat or the world?"

When a cat eats it gobbles, crouched, bunched up as if to spring away from danger at any moment. Its tail lies flat along the floor, the tip curved slightly to the left or right, the direction of flight.

A cat is like a movie. I could say more, but you see the point.

The way a cat looks at the world makes you think it's looking at a movie.

The smooth softness and warmth of a cat is contradicted by its tongue, which is like the surface of a rasp.

Not simply another species, a cat belongs to an order of being different from that of dogs.

When it comes to loneliness, a cat is good company. It is a lonely animal. It understands you and feels what you feel. A dog also understands, but it makes a big deal out of being there for you, bumping against you, flopping about your feet, licking your face. It keeps saying, "Here I am." Your loneliness then feels lugubrious. A cat will just be, suffering with you in philosophical silence.

If a cat were ten pounds heavier, it wouldn't seem cute and it could tear your throat out.

You might go on forever trying to say what a cat is. It can't finally be said. God also transcends definition.

DEAN RIPA

Confessions of a Gaboon Viper Lover

N O SNAKE OF MY childhood mythology was more dreamily considered, nor more sought after by me during my first years of collecting venomous snakes abroad, than the Gaboon viper, whose morphological wonder seemed to fulfill all the dreads—and desires—I had to experience, in line and color the very image of pure Death. Coming upon a Gaboon viper in the grass is like stumbling onto a pile of human bones; it gives you the same sense of shock, of trespass into an unwelcome territory. The pallid oblongs that traverse the animal's spine look like nothing so much as the disconnected articulations of a dismembered skeleton, held in ligaments of hourglasses. A head of cruel pale color, heart-shaped, flat; it might be a blanched tree leaf—or the denuded pate of a human skull half embedded in the forest litter. Left unmolested, the snake is not likely to move, relying on its disruptive pattern to sink indistinguishably into the leaves in front of you. Once startled, however, that stone-dead skeleton stirs with the sudden viciousness of unexpected life! The head heaves abruptly forward like an arrested javelin, and the squat, tire-sized body, blowing up and down like a molten, fluid thing, jerks spastically, the reeded nostrils under the fork-horned nose growling out blasts of air from bloated, twitching coils. The Gaboon viper rises and moves and appears! Like some secret glyph writing in a chaotic code, the ancient warning invoked: *"Halt! Go no further! Here is Death!"*

There is something supremely eerie in the character of this snake's appearance. Like the archetype of a vast human idea that sets gongs going off and warning flags raising, the pattern of the Gaboon viper exploits racial memories of the fear of death itself. Question: If the Gaboon viper is mimetic of something in nature, *what* (in nature) is it mimetic *of?* Why this *particular* design, whose fearful expression—formed some ten million years before man set foot on the scene—communicates images of death and horror to all who behold it?

She is not an ugly snake.* By any artist's standard, she could be called art. Her pattern might have been lifted from a Persian carpet. She crawls in an oriental profusion, richly colored and drawn, her lines evocative of all that is startling and bizarre in nature. Purples, carmines, buffs, mauves, silky white crescents and splashes of green ellipses under a longitude of dun-colored coffin shapes outlined in black, are arrayed in pastel hues on each large spade-shaped scale. Conflicting and fantastic shapes, embedded with cryptic symbols and arcane directives, have been embroidered into her hide, acting on the subconscious level with the nameless fear promptings of certain dreams. Ornate, wonderful and terrible, her forever fashionable design strikes the viewer as forbiddingly as the scarlet hourglass on the abdomen of the black widow spider. Here is something awful, something that

---

*The writer is speaking of his own personal Gaboon, Madame Zsa Zsa.

can kill . . . but there is a loveliness to this Death, a soft, velvety allure. In the tenebrious conditions of its forest environment (walking through true rain forest may be equated with walking on the bottom of the sea—it's that dim) the snake seems an outwardly meaningless shape, part of a background. Behind the verdant stage wires of her theatrical jungle, in a crazy painted domain of mossy and incult avenues, she waits like a deadly potential for conscious perception—to make her *real.*

"The look of *bones* is what makes them so highly coveted," a witch priest in Old Sunyani (Tanzania) told me years after I'd caught my first one. "One can *see* into the pattern . . ." Just what things he *saw* he declined to say. That the Gaboon viper should be revered as a holy object among some African snake cults is not surprising. Among "covetable" creatures, snakes rank high, but certainly few other snakes (and few other animals, excepting certain insects), can compare with the serpents of the *Bitis* group (Gaboons, rhino vipers, puff adders), in the jewel-like perfection of their forms. A Gaboon viper in the exhibition case at a zoological park is apt to magnetize more awestruck faces to the glass than any other, and incur more remarks afterward. How is it that the snake is in *zoo* at all, and not an art museum? The Gaboon viper makes one aware of the feebleness of human art, always imitative of nature. The strongest paintings can little compete with it for sheer effect and impression. An ever-changing, liquid form, it strains the art critic's preposterous theories as to origins. One day it is Kandinsky zigzags, a borderline hallucination; at another moment, with the mere shifting of its coils, it is a litter of bones more compelling than any of Georgia O'Keefe's meretricious skulls. Its colors, a conglomeration of peculiarly African symmetries, seem lifted from an African shield painting. Did I say the beast has horns? I didn't mean this halfheartedly. A pair of forked rhinoceran appendages crown the nose of this otherworldly devil, like a weird afterthought to creation. Nasal appendages seem out of place on a snake; on a heart-shaped nose of enlarged nostrils, pugged like a pig's, they seem a macabre embellishment; something from Bosch's hell world, or Durer's engraving of the Devil in the Garden. Add silvery little eyes that flicker like mica chips in the face, and a tendency to maggot-like bloatedness, and you have a creature incomparably perverse, repellent, and beautiful. The Gaboon viper, queen of the world's deadly maggots, might be a living model for the early Christian demons depicted in the Gothic Renaissance.

To the African native it presents as stark and frightening an appearance as one of their own ancestral Devils made carnate—a breathing, flattening, spreading thing, with horns and eyes glittering on a vaguely human mask, like one of their own grotesque fetish carvings come to life. Violent expellations of breath produce a rasping, growling sound that no prayer to fetishes can propitiate; the body, expanding taut as if to explode, contracts, withers alternately, like some hideous hallucination of a demon being that can both shrink and increase itself at will. The angular head depresses sharply, mashing its nose against the dirt, so that the silvery little cat-like eyes seem bent back into the rubbery flesh of its head. The creature seems to be making horrible Chinese faces at its observer to frighten him away; the huge venom glands, swollen with the amplitude of lethal potentials, displace the angles of its jaws, and are thus enlarged and amplified by these contortions. On some specimens these glands may be tinged a pinkish hue of their own—like the baboon's florid bottom, they scream out at you—pulsing, throbbing against the dirt. . . . Flanking the back of the head, painted in mirrorment on the apex of the glands, are two large black spots that stare out like the eyes of a target, lending a death's head moth appearance to the face. Their position is strangely deceptive, giving the impression that the snake is looking backward at you, even as it looks forward, with the head connected to the "trunk" in reverse! The real eyes are tinier, like vertical slits in the face, set far on the muzzle and hidden within disruptive black arrows invading the lips. The unblinking, jewel-like gaze is not as fixed or immobile as it seems. Now and then, the eyes can be perceived to *twitch* visibly, as with some furtive intention; their movement, at once appraisive and stealthy in the motionless head, conveys a strange intelligence that seems inappropriate, even ghoulish, in an animal that has no arms or legs. Like a devious little humanoid mind imprisoned in glassy cockpits of eyes, the snake appears to be considering your motives. Or plotting some tricky maneuver to steal your soul. . . .

Had the snake any fur, one would have no trouble in accepting it as a mammal—a new line of mammals, maybe, ones who had given up bothering with limbs—a creature well on the road to weasels, rats, and human beings. The horns, the pugged head, the weird little vertical eyes, the slug-like body dressed in the elaborate pattern—on a snake these features seem suspect somehow, part of a costume, a disguise. Here is Madame Zsa Zsa, stretching like taffy through her Halloween jungle, on her way to some nameless ball. . . . *"Who are you?"* you ask, charmed and inspired.

Her discrete hips slink like a flaccid lure into the moonlit
fronds. Implausible, desirable, some indefinable teleology,
present latently, but strongly palpable, makes one question
her very "snakeness." Morphologically, she seems halfway to
some unspeakable transformation that may or may not include a human head. The palaver is finished—with an
abruptness you could never imagine, she is gone—and off
you go without her, despondent and alone, to make water in
the tall grass. Now *here* is the amputated torso of the local
witch priest lying across the footpath, in the process of some
Juju reversion to human form. . . . "Excuse *me!*" you
cry—seeing as it was magic and not love all along—and
stepping quickly over the quixotic shape (so as not incon-
venience his change), you go running back to the hut for
more palm wine.

The Gaboon viper does not yield easily her confidences.
There is no appealing to her human qualities. Her shocking
appearance in the long grass may drive the foraging bush
man to temporary insanity. Impending destruction by his
gods is forthcoming, and he knows it. Something he was not
supposed to see. He may flee, shrieking *"Obeah!"*—having
beheld the very source of his superstitious dreads. As often,
his fears leave him paralyzed in his tracks, sweating bullets
and quite unable to move in the presence of the snake. "I am
hypnotized the way little birds are hypnotized by the stare of
snakes till they can be caught and eaten," his brain squirms,
"Soon he will eat my soul!" This latter talent of snakes (soul
eating) has never been disproved to me, by the way; the for-
mer—that of mesmerism—one may argue, is the result of
fear. I ask instead: what is *fear* but a kind of hypnotic trance?
I have heard more than one African complain of motor

paralysis upon encountering this snake. Others tell of a magnetic draw that reels them irresistibly toward it.

A Ghanaian man, Harry Tembo, confided an interesting story to me while I was undergoing treatment for malaria in Accra. He was out driving in the country, returning from a visit to his less worldly relatives, when, by some hideous magnetism, his car was suddenly *drawn* off the road to collide with a tree! The presence of a Gaboon viper, lying coiled nearby the crashed vehicle, was the sullen proof of ulterior forces at work. "The snake pulled me off the road!" he shouted at me, "It tried to kill me!" "Decidedly," I said to him, putting the *ganja* pipe to my mouth, "Just as it has drawn *me* to your Africa!" I remember a young guide who, before going into a kind of conniption fit in the grass, chanced upon a certain Gaboon viper we had been hunting for several days. He froze in his tracks, his yellow eyes wild and whirling, a mute utterance of terror struggling on his lips, while, below one foot (raised midair), lay the deadly zigzag of familiar coils. His cry was withheld to no purpose: snakes are deaf to airborne sounds. A moment later and the man was flipping and frothing in the leaves. We could never understand the reason for these histrionics, but they seemed sound practice, as no bite had been struck.

There is always this danger when walking in even the most open terrain, that one may tread upon the Gaboon viper unawares. I recall an episode.

A snarl of tree limbs and stick debris from a small land clearing sat heaped in a stack. Eyewitnesses to the snake's proximity were abundant. A half a dozen scared cane workers saw it crawl into the sticks, but never out again. They ran to get the "snake men," naturally, as a bounty had been offered. Clearing the tree limbs by hand, sifting them piece by piece, so as not to miss anything, we were soon left with a cleared, neat circle of flattened grass and leaves—and no snake! For a while we stood disgruntledly about, fuming and talking our "lying" informants down. Two hours work in the African heat for nothing, and both of us malarial! Taking a single step forward (by way of exiting the disappointing premises), a startling blast of air brought the rocketing bump of an unseen head against my shoe. *There* was a young Gaboon viper, hissing like a boiling blast furnace, coiled but scant inches from my foot! It had struck out blindly, close-mouthed, not to bite, but to warn. It had been coiled placidly beside my foot all that time, and we hadn't seen it! Subsequent search with a rake through the dry matted leaves turned up two others—each as undetectable as the first.

"Seeing" the Gaboon viper seems largely participatory, on a parallel with perception itself. Like Dali's paranoiac-critical method of the hidden face, there arises that "magic" effect of audience creation. The eye seeks form and structure, even in the worst chaos. Most people agree that a "car" looks like a car, a "tree" a tree—but this is an *agreement,* it should be remembered, a consensus of like expectations, for there are other truths, other worlds. . . . The Gaboon viper offers no key to unravel her, no solidity, no aspect, only a giddiness and a sense of swarming, a liquidity of incurving circles bending the vision to fish-eyed extremes. This is never more apparent than when one is led out to the scene of a recent snake bite, and expected to turn up a snake.

"We saw it *there.* . . . "

The tribesmen had fear in their eyes. They had taken me over two miles through dense bush, and now they pointed with stark insistence to some obscure region under the trees. A clump of green and brown ferns formed a little island hillock in the swamp, where a rise of palm fronds over a mud pool doted like so many women's skirts trailing mold. An expanse of yellowish flotsam, coagulating in a shaft of sunlight, signified the treacherous nature of the ground surface. Somewhere out there was the snake. . . . It wasn't enough to have to worry about crocodiles lying up hidden, but the murky bog water was inhabited by the schistosoma snail.

"It is just *there*," my man repeated, "Beneath the fronds. . . . Look!"

I *was* looking. . . . Their wondrous African eyes saw everything—I saw *nothing*.

"Look near the stump," suggested another, reaching forth a shaking, nubbed hand (spitting cobra bites and bush medicine, but he is very efficient with the machete even without fingers). "There . . . *now* do you see it?"

The sad truth was that I did not. I saw leaves, fronds, sticks and weeds, nothing more.

"*Onan-ka?*" I asked, trying to confirm if it was Gaboon, and not anxious to wade through any more mud for another harmless *Philothamnus*. "Is it *onan-ka?*"

The tall man nodded with exaggerated gravity, and traced an abstract shape in the air. They led me closer, into an overshadowed distance of withered limbs suspended in a lace of mossy tendrils. Their faces spasmed against the insects striking their eyes. We had approached so closely now that the men had become visibly afraid. Yet still I saw *nothing*.

"There . . . *see! see!*" they blurted hastily, anxious to be gone from the place.

My men were losing faith in me. "This white snake man

is either blind or stupid!" I could hear them thinking, "—or so scared he pretends to be!"

"It is *there!*" exclaimed their group leader, in a low, hissing tone. His eyes darted around as though fearful of phantom betrayals. "How is it that you cannot perceive it?"

"Come . . . come . . . " whispered another, "We will go the other way, from behind!"

This new path was even deeper and more obscure. We found ourselves sinking up to our knees in places. Black leeches mobbed our legs. In a panic, we sought out the higher, dry ground, stumbling up onto crumbling logs. When I looked back the leeches were somersaulting after us! A lit cigarette applied to their flabby, detestable surfaces, and they released their numbing hold, leaving bloody trails behind them on our skin. We penetrated further, till at length the way became impassable. Now on hands and knees we crawled, worming out way into brush tangles, careful where to place our fingers, for the ground was alive with black ants. Venomous green vines dangled against us from the thickets above; we snaked on our bellies, cowering, shrinking from hidden, nettled things that pricked and stabbed, from a curious powder that rained like spores down into our hair and eyes. We came at last to a vaulted area, where flabby leafed plants flanked a spacious overhang above our heads. Here we were able to stand upright for once. A natural arbor, or tunnel, as if the woods had parted around an immense lozenge-shaped object that had bulldozed its way through, made a natural ceiling above us. Declivities big as barrel heads splayed the mud just ahead—the cavernous spoor of the bush elephant.

"*It is there* . . . now you *must* see it!" The two men were wriggling and pointing, their black hides shining with sweat, their mouths gaping with exhaustion and a horror that they had allowed themselves to come so close. We were evidently almost up on top of it. But *where* was it?

I didn't dare ask them again.

Rather than try their nerves any further, risk them deserting me in a depth of wilderness I little knew the way out of, I started blindly off alone in the direction they indicated, my snake hook winnowing the weeds in front of me, my ears harkening for the violent hiss I hoped would come before the broad wedge-shaped head shot out from nowhere, falling like an axe blade against my leg.

"*There! . . . there! . . . there!*" the men shrieked behind me.

I looked down.

It was true. The Gaboon was there, smiling vexedly up at me, fat as a car tire under the tangled fronds. Its coil was such that it filled and overflowed one of the elephant tracks, a sleeping pile of evil crisscrosses looking up with silvery eyes. Nearly three hours since they'd spotted it, and it hadn't budged a purple inch.

Coming upon a Gaboon viper under the dim tree canopy, seeing it literally materialize before you from the debris of the forest floor, is perhaps the closest one can ever come among live creatures to the fright of encountering an actual ghost.

ANN ROWER

The Crying Jag

R EMEMBER," MARCHELLE said after we got home
from the library, "last year when your cousin Jerry
called after Wendee killed herself and asked you if
you wanted the cat and I said take it, take it cause I thought
he meant the Jaguar?"

My obsession with the Jaguar was famous. Marchelle
shared it and we joked about it constantly. We went to the library to find more information, especially the kind that
would somehow justify our love, cause we always adored the
big cats, but especially jags. They were so strong, so tough,
so fast, or so I thought until that day at the library, where it
turns out that jaguars are not the fastest cat in the West.
They have big chests and short stocky legs, which slows
them down, making them slower than cheetahs and
cougars, though cougars are more of a mid-range, cheaper.
But they love the water and love to swim and they also climb
trees and wait. Adorable! Another reason I always loved the
animal was that they seemed, especially the one on the car,
so sleek and yet so female. In the library, Webster's III said
the name for a true jaguar is jagurare(t)te. Purr-fect! According to the *Encyclopedia of World Animals*: "If the Puma
is the Lion of the New World, the Jaguar (panthera onca) is

the Leopard. . . . the largest and fiercest American carni-
vore, the jaguar shows no fear of people, unlike the Puma
and may even become a man [I believe the correct term is
now people] eater. It does much harm and is hunted relentlessly.

"The jaguar, also called el tigre, is the biggest cat in
America. In those days the jaguar was native to the area as far
north as the Red River in Arkansas. Some debatable records
say its explosive, snarling roar was known and feared as far
east as the Carolinas. Because the early Spaniards placed a
bounty on it, the jaguar was almost wiped out by the 1800s.
One was reported in New Mexico in 1903, and an occasional
animal still wanders across the border, but the species is all
but gone from the states." As I read on, it became clear that
all the jaguar stuff, in North America anyway, is in the past
tense and the book itself ain't that new either. So, with a mys-
teriously sinking feeling, I went deeper and deeper into the
reference room. Somehow I had a feeling something terrible
happened to the jaguar. I look in the *Readers Guide* and the
New York Times index. I look under Jaguar.

> Save the cat.
> The law of the jungle catches up with the jaguar.
> Would you pay $2 billion for a sick cat.

It's all so sad.

> Jaguar's trying to beat the heat.
> The nine lives of the jaguar.
> New breed focuses on transformation of the jaguar.

This is seeming a little more upbeat, though I'm not sure what transformation means here. Maybe it's like the South Florida panther thing, where there're so few of them that in-breeding is weakening the already nearly extinct species. So they're bringing the cougars in and letting them inter-breed—shocking! Or, as the researcher being interviewed said, "surely not the first thing we try in 'recovery.'" I didn't know they had recovery groups for animals. What are they called, AAA? Anyway, my heart is lifting a bit about the future of the planet, but then there's nothing in 1989 at all. Extinction. More on Mick Jagger and Japan, which jaguar's in between. In 1988, there's half a page on Jesse Jackson, though.

> Jaguar says its sales will fall again this year
> after dropping by 10% in 1990.
> SEE ALSO AUTO

I'm crushed. I feel like a fool. I can't believe it. All this time I thought they were talking about the animal. Why, then, do I feel just as sad? There is in fact only one reference to jaguar, the animal, and it says:

> SEE ALSO ZOO

It's a story about a two-hundred-pound jaguar who pushed open the door of its cage and ate its brother's keeper. Marchelle sees my sadness.

"Why are you so sad?"

I explain about the jaguar being a sick cat.

"I'm sure there are plenty of healthy jaguars roaming about in the wild," she says.

"Not in the *Readers Guide*," I say.

"What ever happened to that Jag?" Marchelle asked.

Memories! The time Jerry, my cousin Wendee's father, called to tell me she had killed herself, it was the first time he ever called me. Then, a couple of days later he called again. After not speaking ever on the phone for years, he calls twice in that many days. My first thought was that the second call was more bad news. Marcie, Wendee's mother, had died of grief or some such, but noooooo. He was calling to offer me Wendee's cat, Grizzabella (from *Cats*—you know, the one who sings "Memories" . . .). I loved Griz. She was beautiful, a strange breed as far as color and markings: a mute calico, the variety was called. Not that she didn't talk. In fact, that one time I had a successful visit with her she was very sweet and very talkative. No, the mute had to do with her color. She was a long-hair calico, white with orange and grey, only the orange and grey were very pale, muted.

They've been doing a lot of research just this year on coloration in animals and how the leopard got its spots. It's a question of a peptide and a hormone and timing and switches, a default switch, like a computer, activates brown and if it's on too long, black, and then an override allows little granules of yellow or orange pigment to attach themselves, like little gifts on a Christmas tree, to the hair follicles. Actually, the peptides act like combination ushers and stimulants, increasing production and guiding to the right place at the same time. And you know what? Those same peptides and hormones also influence reproductive development and the production of endorphins. You think gen-

tlemen prefer dumb blondes but the thing is, it's the gentle-
men who are dumb. The blondes are deaf. Lots of other de-
fects too. Even natural blondes are unnatural. At least that's
what they've found when the override switch is on too long
and allows too many yellow or orange particles to adhere to
the hair shaft. I always suspected that. How many big sloppy
floppy golden retrievers do you know? Or big stupid clown-
ish orange tabbies? I bet lots. One night our big dumb
much-beloved orange tabby Stuart dropped (literally, I
think, from the edge of our sleeping loft, I mean how dumb
can you get?) dead in the middle of the night at only fourteen months. We heard a crash. I thought it was a lamp. I
came down. It was Stuart, taking his last breath, eyes and
mouth open just a little bit, like almost slack, and Josefina,
his sister, standing above him, tail three inches in diameter,
hair standing straight up all down her spine and eyes as
wide as full moons. We never knew what happened. The vet
said SDS (sudden death syndrome—not something you
want to have happen too often) but I always suspected Josefina pushed him. He got all that attention. But I didn't write
that murder mystery story because I know Gary doesn't
want any more stories about cats and dogs. He told Vito so.

What do you expect, man? V said. All your friends live in
the city? You think they're gonna write about horses and
cows? Or snakes? Or chickens?

So I thought, well, there goes my idea to write "What
Josefina Saw," the story of how I would never be able to know
what happened and how I only wished that I could somehow
know what Josefina saw, and began to suspect that somehow,
she'd had a paw in it maybe, catricide and that made me

think about Grizzy and what she saw that night that Wendee died.

Anyway, so it's not blonde but brown which is the peak form color, especially in the agouti pattern—agouti, a giant hundred-pound rodent, is right up there with jaguars' favorite lunch meat. The agouti pattern is the coloration pattern they've studied the most—brown hair shaft with orange or yellow in the middle and black tip. It's the brown that comes from the most perfect functioning of these colorizing functions in the body and brain. And that explains something to me, one of the first things I noticed about L.A. culture that seemed so different from Eastern style. Several years ago, on one of my first visits to my new (by marriage) L.A. family, Chadnie, who was my Aunt Cherry's great granddaughter, was four and we were talking—natch—about cars, cause Aunt Cherry must have just gotten her new antelope Jaguar then. I remember thinking, before I started doing my research, that it was perverse to name the color of her car "antelope" when that was the jaguar's favorite food. I had an image of the antelope once it was ingested somehow staining all the way through to the exterior and giving it its color. Then I found out that jaguars don't eat antelope at all. And then I found out that the antelope (the pronghorn antelope of North America anyway) is the fastest animal on earth, so maybe the manufactures were trying to do another of those recombinant things by naming the Jaguar "antelope." Although one book said its favorite food is horses, mostly they either fish or eat little piglike creatures which when I saw the picture made me laugh. They just really look like giant mice. How cute. They're called pessaries, I think, or is that the name of the stuff Orthodox Jewish men wrap around their testicles on the Sabbath? No. Actually, the two favorite foods of the jaguar are peccaries and capybaras and one article in the *New York Times* referred to capybaras as "rutabagas of the animal world . . . a big ball of flab."

Anyway, I remember we were playing and I asked Chadnie what color car she wanted when she grew up.

"Brown," she lisped.

I thought that was so weird a choice for a four year old. What kid, especially a little girl, wants brown? Red, yes, or blue, maybe. I always liked blue. But brown? And then I realized, that trip, how many brown cars there were, especially all the rich ladies in Beverly Hills, all these strange shades of brown, some silvery brown, or golden brown, lots of metallic, or pastel browns mixed with cream, which we'd now probably call cappuccino, or, for the deeply cool, latte, even some deep rich chocolatey browns, saturated with color, called Hershey, or fudge. But only now, reading the latest research, do I realize that brown is not just a color to associate with dirt or shit, but with the highest forms of human production, eggs and sperm and endorphins—sex and drugs. This is what I learned about stripes but I suppose spots and "blotches" are also a question of switches and timing. Leopards' spots are rosettes, four or five black blotches in a circle. Panthers are black leopards—not leopards without spots but whose blackness covers, or "coats" the spots. And jaguars, always my favorite, have rosettes of four or five black dots and then a big black rosette in the center. It was such a revelation to me when Marchelle pointed out that the jaguar spot pattern was exactly the same as a paw print all over the outside. That's a very beautiful image, as if their insides and outsides are one, or as if the tracks they leave on the earth are also all over their body. Who leaves those markings?

Anyway, I refused to take Grizzy. In fact, Jerry called me before he called anyone else to ask if I would take her because I was one of the two people on earth she wasn't terrified of and one of them, her "person" (now the correct term, according to animal activists, for what used to be thought of as master or owner of a pet, which as everyone now knows is called an animal companion) had just killed herself. I said no partly because I imagined that Grizzy had just been so traumatized that I couldn't bear the thought of them having to crate her up, tranquilize and send her three thousand miles in a box in the freight compartment of a transcontinental jet: I mean Grizzy had not only been there years through Wendee's depression and Prozac-induced suicide by insect poison—an idea inspired by a Danielle Steele novel she was reading the last time I saw her alive—but sat with the dying and then dead body at least fourteen or sixteen hours before anyone else came, at which point she crawled under the dust ruffle and hid there for a week; and partly because Easter, my own cat buddy of almost twenty-one years, had died days before; and partly because I was pissed, still, from Wendee getting Aunt Cherry's Jaguar and not me. Actually, my fantasy that some day the Jaguar would be mine really began while they were both still alive, one year when Aunt Cherry and I were driving around a lot—I was driving because she'd had too much wine a lot—and she confessed that she didn't really like driving it. It was too hard to handle.

"I'm too old for a sports car," she said.

She'd wanted a European car, a sports car, before she died. She got a Jag, the Vandenplas, the XJ6, burled mahogany interior with sheepskin on the floor—one recently killed by a jaguar, maybe (I found out another of the jaguar's favorite foods is ruminants). "Jaguars will tackle beasts as big as domestic cows and will fight, kill, and devour alligators. They also catch fish: lying in wait on a low branch or river bank, and using a front paw to flip the fish from the water." Cute! But Aunt Cherry was never really happy with her Jaguar. It was too much car. "Though jaguars climb trees, fully grown adults are too heavy to be really agile climbers— they may weigh over 300 pounds and grow to more than eight feet including a two-foot tail. The magnificent jaguar is nearly as strong as a lion and will drag a horse or cow a long way over rough terrain to a sheltered spot where it can eat undisturbed." She missed all the automation of her Sedan de Ville, which Marcie had given her when Jerry bought her her Mercedes. Aunt Cherry'd driven Caddys most of her life. Jerry'd always driven Porsches until recently, when he switched to Mercedes for the long commutes and to match his wife. The Eldorado and then the later Sedan de Ville was completely automated. It practically made ice for you, though she'd completely stopped drinking, meaning one glass at dinner instead of starting a new bottle every day at five P.M. "Jaguars have few natural enemies but sometimes peccary herds are said to corner and kill them. Jaguars are hunted where they prey on domestic animals and are also shot for their beautiful skins." It happened the very first time I was alone with the Jaguar, the day of Aunt Cherry's (it turned out to be last) pedicure. She made an appointment for me to have one—it was my first. But the only time he could squeeze me in was an hour before her, so I would have to drive the Jag there myself and she would come later with Marcie. Beast that she was, Aunt Cherry sensed my fear.

"What are you afraid of?" she crooned sleepily.

"What if something happens to the car?"

"Nothing will happen. What could happen? You've driven it forever."

I jingled my keys in a goodbye wave and shuddered as the skin of a totally different person, one with a Jaguar, slipped around me. I was not enough of an Angeleno to know that a Jaguar was not a totally cool car for a starving artist. A Dodge Dart with a Slant 6 engine that I got off some guy who lived in the Valley for eight hundred bucks would have been more like it, but I just loved the Jaguar for its beauty and power and because although it was not fast and guzzled gas, it loved to swim. I love to swim. "The jaguar swims well, even when burdened with a tapir between its jaws. It fishes in a leisurely manner." I fish. It was fast but not that fast. I was fast but not that fast. I always came in second in the Fourth of July races. I did my errands and went back to Alton, off Burton Way, where I'd parked. Tim Leary, coincidentally—my Tim, not the baseball player—lived on that street. I didn't know the number but he was nowhere to be seen. I thought maybe we'd have a reunion. I wondered if he'd remember me from all those years ago at Harvard. I drove "my" Jag home and waved cavalierly at the doorperson, who greeted me expectantly, ready to open the door, help me out, and valet park me in Aunt Cherry's car as he always did her. She never parked her car herself. But I couldn't get my seat belt unfastened. The motion of pulling up, braking, lowering the window and undoing the belt is a precision move. I was ashamed, but rather than letting him reach in and undo me and then laugh with the other parkers behind my back, I waved him away, like, don't you know I'm too cool to have you park me? I park myself. I zoomed down into the basement garage, where I'd never been—Aunt Cherry always also had the car brought up—and slid the Jag into Aunt Cherry's spot, feeling a huge relief. Without any problem, the seat belt opened, as if it had come unfastened by itself. I had done it. I had lost my fear. I was home. The Jag was home. I did it. It was a transformation, the one I'd devoutly fished, I mean wished. I was one with my beloved Jaguar, I could again dream that she someday would be mine.

The door closed with that fabulous thump, that dead sound that really good car doors make. My heart thumped with pleasure. I turned to give my Jag a last loving glance when my heart stopped completely. The Jag had been "keyed" all along the driver's side. The key mark went all along the driver's side, front fender, front door, back door, rear fender, a silver wound in the silver-brown finish so deep it bled. How could I have not noticed it if it was there before? I rationalized that it could have been because when I took the Jag out, I called down to the desk and the valet parking guy brought it up for me and was already holding that door open. So it might have been there. But I didn't remember noticing it when I parked on Alton. Maybe I was too busy looking at my newly polished toes. I never had red toes. Tim Leary must have done it. I gasped silently and felt more than slightly terrible. My first impulse was not to say anything about it but sometimes you're so upset that you can't lie, you're so desperate for release that even punishment is better than nothing and certainly the wild hope of exoneration— they'll say, oh it's been there for forever—makes me confess.

(I loved the way Marcie and Aunt Cherry used "forever," in a kind of cute way, like they put hearts on their *i*'s instead of dots.) But no one said that. Marcie gasped almost as loudly as I had. I knew in those circles, keying a car—requiring a many-thousand-dollar paint job if you're fussy and most people who own fifty-nine-thousand-dollar cars seem to be fussy—is like being cruel to animals. Aunt Cherry seemed to just smile. The Valium? She thought maybe the men who valet park the cars in the building had done it for spite. She said they sit in her car and smoke pot. She can smell it. With her new hairdo, she seemed much more articulate. Anyway she wasn't mad at me at all. I even offered to pay for it.

"Don't be silly," she cooed. "Wendee is getting the Jag when I die and she can have the key mark fixed then."

Aunt Cherry's reference to her own death hit me hard. I felt a surge of grief, mingled with humor and respect at her remark and then, a grand mal seizure of disappointment like, oh really? You're not willing me the Jag? I felt so genuinely innocently cheated. The Jaguar felt so like mine, especially now that I had maimed it, marked it. In addition to the disappointment, though, I was in shock that the keying incident wasn't played up. The absence of anger, or fuss, was potent. Death put things in perspective in a funny way, I guess.

The next time I saw her, Wendee confessed to me she didn't really like driving Aunt Cherry's Jag either, which made me feel even worse. It felt like an old ladies car to her, or rather that was how it was read by her peers. So important. Old ladies with bleached hair who lived in Beverly Hills drove Vandenplases, or maybe it was like she was riding around inside the old skin or the ghost of Aunt Cherry, who she never got along with and who besides was dead. Worse.

Like Aunt Cherry'd put a curse on Wendee willing her the Jag. Besides, the car was just too feminine for Wendee's new androgyny. Wendee, or Wendyn as she called herself that year, wanted a Miata. I remember that year they only made them in red, white and blue. She wanted a red one but Jerry thought the Jag was more protection, which made her hate and fear it more, I imagine. Because a big powerful car that you're not at ease driving is false protection. That kind of protection, like the Armed Response security systems, just added to the fear instead of taking it away, the same way the fact that everybody wanted jaguars just made them carnivores, killers, and worse, ultimately, extinct. It really was an unlucky car. No wonder I was the only one who ended up wanting it. Maybe because it was I who hurt it so bad. Wendee got sick after she got the Jaguar. One time we were eating out on the terrace of the Brentwood California Pizza. It was fucking November and freezing. She ordered three entrees and hardly ate any of them. What sickness is that? Everything looks so good on the menu you can't decide? And then when they come there's so much food that you lose your appetite? Is there a name for that? Phood phobia? I realized later that the reason we'd had lunch alfresco—I was alfreddo—was her claustrophobia.

She asked me, "Why did my grandmother (meaning Aunt Cherry) hate me?"

"She didn't hate you," I said. I didn't tell her that Aunt Cherry had said to me that she didn't like Wendee because Wendee wasn't tough enough. She was too sensitive. But I didn't say that. "She gave you her Jaguar," I said, trying to keep the pout out of my tone.

But after her suicide I was dying of curiosity about when

they fixed the key mark and what happened to the Jag, since
it had not been offered to me. I was especially interested in
when the key mark got fixed and how much it cost, still feeling guilty, still surprised that Aunt Cherry hadn't had it sent
in for repairs immediately, right when it happened. After all,
she was still making pedicure appointments. But I forgot
that Aunt Cherry died only four days after the Jag got keyed
so it was understandable. My fault? At that time I certainly
didn't make a connection then between the keying of the Jag
and Aunt Cherry's death. And at first when Wendee got sick
right after she got the Jag, I didn't think about that either,
and never even noticed the next time I came out because
Wendee wasn't driving much and my few hints about using
the car fell on deaf ears and I didn't want to bring it up too
much because I was afraid they were still secretly mad about
the keying even though it was never expressed. But after she
died, it seemed so crass to ask about it, like how I kept wanting to ask Jerry to show me Wendee's suicide note but didn't
know the etiquette.

But finally, this one day driving around in the rain, I did
ask Marcie what happened to the Jag. The rain really was the
reason because the rain reminded her of another rainy day,
years ago, and that in turn gave me my in.

"I can't tell you the year. When was my new Jag? Eighty-
four? Chadnie was five. I locked my keys in the car. Maybe
Wendee was sick then too. We always had Cadillacs before
that and we put the extra key under the wheel well. I didn't
know what to do. I told someone. Go call a taxi. I asked her
to wait with my groceries. I ran and came back as fast as I
could and waited by the car, sitting and shivering, afraid to
leave. I had come to Westward Ho, a market always full of

celebrities from the Palisades. They had separate turkey parts. It was for Leo. He loved the thigh. Finally the taxi came and I looked at the time and I realized that if he took me home to get my extra keys and brought me back, Westward Ho would be closed. It didn't used to stay open twenty-four hours. So he says what do you need and I explained I locked my money in the car too and he says don't worry so he runs in and gets the turkey thighs and drives me home to Bel-Air and waits and I run in and get my keys and give the turkey thighs to Marta to put in the refrigerator and the taxi cab driver rides me back to the Palisades and it's pouring, April, just like today. That's the only time I took a taxi in my life. Then I got in an accident and smashed up the Jag."

"I didn't know you had a Jag," I said, blown away by the complexity of the story I'd just heard. I mean what was the subtext of that tale? Uncle Leo liked "the thigh"? Why did it seem such a revelation that Marcie had a Jag? Was that why Aunt Cherry wanted one? I guess there is that turning point in life when mothers start imitating their daughters.

"Yes. I always had Jaguars."

I tried to get up my nerve to bring up the real burning question of this visit: what happened to Aunt Cherry's antelope Jaguar which she gave to Wendee after Wendee committed suicide? I guess I was still suffering from the disappointment that they didn't offer it to me, that they only offered me the cat, though actually my refusal to take Grizzabella was the best thing that could have happened to her, because now Grizzy had her own room, with her food, water and litter box, as well as the kids' kindergarten drawings, Uncle Leo's old file cabinet, Jerry's golf clubs—what we'd call a storage room in the East but in this house, it was the room the alarm system called the Memory Room, fitting because Wendee's favorite song was "Memories," from *Cats*, whence Grizzy got her name.

Anyway, back to the Jag. I'd soothed myself thinking one of the other "kids" must have gotten it. In their family, cars were always passed down, the assumption being that the younger the family member the more they could use the more expensive car of the elder, though Randi and Dorean both had bigger Mercedes than Marcie and Jerry, their parents. Scott had a Porsche like his dad always had till now, practically, except for those two last Mercedes. Maybe they'd put it in storage so Chadnie could have it when she was sixteen. She was already ten.

"What happened," I said, very hesitantly, "to Wendee's Jag? I mean Aunt Cherry's Jag—" (my Jag, I thought) and as soon as I said it I was sorry. Me and my big mouth. Why can't I learn to keep it closed? I knew it would remind her of Wendee and I was afraid it would remind her of that day when her mother was dying and the car got keyed when I was driving it, but the question just popped out.

"Yes, remember the day it got keyed?" she said, not saying anything about my being responsible for it. That absence of affect about the incident was still so affecting.

"There was no one in the family who wanted it and there was nothing to trade it in for so we just sold it to a second-hand dealer."

"You didn't even have it repainted?" I said, astounded.

"No."

"And Wendee never had the key mark fixed?"

She started to cry but she did not stop driving.

"No. She said she didn't care."

I winced. Another measure of the pathology of West L.A. depression. And suddenly now, driving around in this rare Southern California downpour and what with the tears in Marcie's eyes, the key mark which I used to see as a big long jagged mark along one side like a big sharp claw mark by an L.A. jaguarette who'd just had her manicure, turned, in my mind, into a big long horizontal tear stain—you know the way a tear marks its path down a little kid's dirty face—like the car was crying, not bleeding. I forever now thought of that beautiful antelope brown beast that I loved and coveted so relentlessly and never got as the CRYING JAG.

"She was too sick."

"You didn't fix it for her?"

"No."

"You didn't even fix it before you sold it?"

"No. We just sold it to a used-car dealer. It was a lousy deal but we didn't care."

I looked at her. Her eyes were brimming, then her face was wet as the windshield as we turned onto Wilshire and sailed past the VA Hospital.

"See! I told you," she said, changing the subject bravely. She pointed to the big green lawn of the VA Hospital on Wilshire and Veteran.

She had told me how she'd driven past the government building yesterday and they were watering the lawn. The government was supposed to make the rules and there they were, watering their grass in the pouring rain while L.A. was still in the worst drought in thirty years and Marcie and Jerry weren't even allowed to wash their cars or clean their pools and got fined by Cal Gas if they didn't cut back their water.

"Like, we had to turn off the automatic system and now

you're only allowed to water when you need to. I mean, you have to go out and feel it. How can you tell? And the VA runs theirs in the middle of a thunderstorm. I'm going to call somebody!"

We drove on.

"Look. There's some more. Sprinklers!"

But I smiled. One of my favorite things—like flames in sunlight—is fountains in the rain.

"No," Marcie said, going back to the Jaguar. "Nobody wanted it."

I kept my trap shut.

BARBET SCHROEDER

Koko, A Talking Gorilla

T HE FILM ABOUT Koko came about like this: I heard about someone who'd gone into a zoo where a gorilla was sick, in the nursery. That person, Penny Patterson, had volunteered to start teaching sign language to the gorilla. (Since the gorilla was sick, she couldn't take it to the university.) A relationship developed between the gorilla and this student, who was applying research that had been done before with chimpanzees. It had never been done with a gorilla. She later obtained permission to move her project onto the Stanford campus.

What attracted me was the dramatic, rather than the scientific, side: that the zoo, after a couple of years, was ready to send the police to get the gorilla back, because Penny didn't want to give it back. The gorilla was the property of the zoo.

So I took a plane, and went to study the situation. As soon as I saw what was going on, I knew this was a great subject. I decided to make a movie. Over the next few years, I studied the sign language and visited Koko very often, and wrote a treatment. The documentary, *Koko, A Talking Gorilla,* was a preparation for a feature, but the feature never got made.

A gorilla foundation was formed. They bought the go-

135

rilla from the zoo in the end. There was a very close bond between Koko and Penny Patterson. Koko was seeing mostly females; the volunteers were almost all women, so I was one of the rare male presences around Koko. Koko had one of her first sexual experiences with me. I noticed one day she was masturbating against my leg. My blue jeans got quite wet.

Not only did Koko understand that she was being filmed, she learned how to start the camera very, very quickly. She has this big sausage hand, and to start an Eclair camera, you have this tiny little switch. She would behave differently the minute the camera was rolling, and after a while she would even walk by the camera and start it. It was amazing.

The camera made a little noise when it was rolling, and she saw there was a change in attitude in everyone when the camera was on. I guess she kind of liked that.

She became like an actress. I cannot say that she did things for the camera, but she was performing more, yes.

Koko has real star quality. She's someone who's fascinating to watch, whatever she does. The way she moves, the way she does things, she has some kind of extraordinary natural elegance. When I watch big stars, that's also what fascinates me. She has a real screen presence. Marlon Brando, or Idi Amin Dada, have that kind of presence. That was one element. The other element was that this was the first time in a scientific experiment that you could prove you were actually communicating with a non-human individual. That was very moving. You cannot define a "person" only by the fact that it's human. A person is something that's conscious of itself in time and space.

Koko had a vocabulary of several hundred words of human language. She is definitely conscious of herself in time. Is she a person? Does she have rights?

I haven't kept in touch with the people at the Gorilla Foundation. When I do a movie, it's like a love affair. Then it disappears and I move on to the next.

There were many attempts with a male, Michael, to induce Koko to have children. The idea was that the Gorilla Foundation wanted to watch and see if Koko and Michael would teach sign language to their children. Every attempt was made to have Michael and Koko have sex. But the gorillas are not very sex-oriented. They have very little penises. They tried everything, including showing them porno movies of gorillas fucking in a zoo. Koko and Michael were interested, the sounds got them a little excited, but not enough to inspire them to do the same.

The film was done over a period of a year, 1977.

The life span of a gorilla is fifty years. Koko was still very young, and not very heavy. Now she's doubled her size.

The philosophical questions are interesting. What is a person? What is language? What is communication? Koko's situation raised all the most important questions.

Jean-Pierre Gorin made his film about the "secret language" twins, *Poto and Cabengo,* at about the same time. There was something about both these films that had to do with a kind of freak California situation. The films are parallel on that level: about language, and about a kind of freak situation. It sounded more like a California story than an American one.

Initially, the zoo argued that we were depriving the taxpayers' children in San Francisco of a gorilla to watch. At the hearings, a lot of children came to support Koko's right not to be put back in the zoo. We had the children show that they didn't want Koko in the zoo. The hearing was an endless, ongoing thing. I tried instead to concentrate on the phenomenon and its philosophical implications.

I'm curious. I like to explore different zones. I don't see any relationship between this film and my others. I'm an explorer. I'm sure there are relationships, but it's not for me to say.

This was the first time I had a strong fascination with an animal, because it was the first time I dealt with an animal who told me things: that she did not want the yellow sweater to go out, but the red one. And the red one was not in the room. She was signing what she wanted. This was very moving, to be dealing with somebody who was so much a person. I became a fanatic for gorillas. I ended up going to Africa and seeing where they were. And the horrible things that were happening. People didn't realize that not only were there only a few hundred gorillas left, but that those animals were persons. They each have a different personality. In our society, a person has rights. So this opens all kinds of moral questions.

I got very involved. I went to see a man who had about ten or twenty gorillas in a giant cage. He was going in and having fun with them. But it's very dangerous to play with a gorilla. They can kill you without even knowing it. I had a long love story with gorillas that will go on for the rest of my life.

There are only a few hundred left. Now there's a civil war where they live, and there's nobody to protect them. Sometimes they're killed by poachers, sometimes just for food. When you see that it's happening, educating the people there is extremely difficult—the people are starving, how can you explain that they can't grow things on the land of the goril-las? It's a horrible situation. The gorillas are chased higher and higher into the volcanoes, where there's fog all the time, so they catch pneumonia. When we got close to them in the fog, they were all coughing, because they've been chased so far into the mountains.

That's why Diane Fossey was such a fanatic. She was in contact with an unbearable reality. Her only way was to threaten to shoot anybody who tried to come near the goril-las. I wrote to her, saying I would like to come and talk to her, and she answered, "Don't even try to come near my camp; I'll shoot you." And she was right. When I understood what was happening, I agreed that it was the only way to do it. But of course, that was the last stand. Now things are getting much worse than anything she had dreamt in her worst nightmares.

There are no structures to protect these gorillas. In a civil war, there's nobody there to protect them. It's like the Angkor Wat temples in Cambodia. Everybody's walking in there and taking pieces. Soon the only gorillas left will be the ones in captivity, and to make them reproduce is very com-plicated. It's a sad story, because they're so close to us. There's less than .01 percent difference in the blood, amino acids and all that. Almost no difference.

HUNT SLONEM

For the Birds

I T STARTED WHEN I was about ten, with parakeets. There were always limitations put on me by my parents. We moved a lot; I could only collect so many birds. The next bout of collecting birds had to do with being in the tropics. When I was sixteen I was an exchange student in Nicaragua, the family I lived with had a pet parrot, and I bought some birds in the marketplace. That was the first time I had an experience with a toucan, in Managua in 1969. Then I went to school in Mexico in 1971 and went berserk there, I used to cut classes to go to the marketplace to buy painted buntings. So that's where it started, and then it subsided for many years.

I moved to New York. One night I'd made some money from some prints, and I was walking down Broadway past this place that had amazing finches. I'd never seen anything like it: purple grenadiers and star finches and Peter twin-spots, these extraordinary-looking things. It would've been cheaper to get addicted to heroin at that point. A thousand dollars a week on finches. I had this big cage built, and got all excited about that. I had some problems around 1980. It's a tremendous responsibility, you don't just go away and lock the door, it's very expensive. I figure now it takes about

$12,000 a year to maintain my birds. It's probably the same price as putting a child through college, but at least I don't have to worry about them getting jobs.

These are my pets and models, they really do earn their keep—you know, when something happens, a sale because of a certain bird. Asian orioles have just done wonders for my work. Anyway, I was able to get the Bronx Zoo to take my first New York collection, because they were very interested in African weavers and I had about fourteen kinds. They couldn't get certain ones I had. I've done deals with institutions where they'll take the rest of the collection because they want a specific thing.

I got hooked on turtles at one point, I had twenty-five turtles, one was a hairy-backed turtle, I paid sixty dollars for it; I got a call six months later saying they wanted it back, it was worth $3,000, they sent it by mistake from Singapore. I said, "Forget it. It's dead." The Turtle Back Zoo in New Jersey heard about it somehow, so I got them to take that and some other things as well. I was able to save all these turtles from Chinatown from becoming soup, which upsets me to no end. I think it's because in Islam or something they consider turtles sacred. There are actually turtle ponds or temples in the Middle East where the turtles are extinct in nature, but they've been in these sacred ponds for so long that they're still thriving there. I have some carry-over of the idea of the sacredness of animals.

I like the idea of rescuing things. I consider myself this harbor for unwanted birds. I get calls periodically. One month I was getting offered incredible things—macaws and toucans, some of my best birds have been cast-off pets. I find that most parrots have a span of ten years keeping people amused, then the people get married or have a kid or break up with someone, and then they want to get rid of it. I seem to be the one they come to.

I pride myself on the fact that most of my birds were born in captivity. I had a show in California, and went to this place called Bell Birds. I got just mesmerized by this green hunting parrot, the most beautiful thing I ever saw. They ended up trading me birds for paintings. They imported birds, the zoos bought from them, they bred them and I got some of the offspring.

My birds live for a long time. Birds often live much longer in captivity than in the wild. Bell Birds had a hummingbird that lived for eight years, and their life expectancy in nature is two years. Several of my birds have already outlived all their owners. Arturo has outlived three people already; he's forty years old. He's a blue and gold macaw. They can live to one hundred. I'm not really what's called a hookbill addict. I like what are called soft-billed birds, which are non–seed-eating birds, exotic things like trouvilles and tanagers and hornbills and lilac rollers, toucans, and barbacks. I love the sounds they make. People say, "How can you live with all these birds? It's so noisy." But listen to this traffic. Aren't the birds pleasanter than that siren going by?

The only ones that drive me nuts, cockatoos really get out of control with noise. Now I understand why they shoot them in Australia; they're driven to it.

Birds are really smart. One of mine says the most amazing things. They're discovering that African grays are as intelligent as dolphins. They are supposed to be as smart as three-year-old humans, whatever that means. Another great thing about all this animal keeping for the past twenty years, a lot of endangered species cannot be re-released into their natural environments because they don't exist anymore, but they breed very easily in captivity. I read about Victorian bird keeping—it's so nauseating, they were so hideous to their animals. Now there's a real reverence for the intelligence and feelings of these creatures. There's a lot of really spoiled birds around.

A lot of people are into bird keeping. They know how to take care of them in ways that prolong their lives rather than shorten them.

Birds are as varied as people. Often domestically raised birds bond to you. They don't think they're birds, they think they're people. I encourage the birds who come here to bond with each other, because you just cannot give them all they want. Some of mine would like to be on my shoulder twenty-four hours a day.

I had two macaws that were very tame pets, and they came here, now they're a bonded pair. Macaws bond for life. They're monogamous; if somebody shoots their mate in the wild they never remarry.

My space is about three thousand square feet, and a fifth of it is used by the birds. Some of them fly all over it, so there's a little bit of shared space. They're in a forty-foot cage that I made out of wire. It's divided into sections according to personalities—who gets along with whom. Sometimes birds will get along for eight years and suddenly I wake up and somebody has a bloody head one morning. I have to move him. They're very territorial. It's a survival-of-the-fittest thing going on. But the birds that're loose, there's plenty of room for them to fly away from each other. Koko, the big macaw, sort of rules the roost. He won't let Arturo anywhere near his turf.

I think this has been therapy for me. I live alone. It's nice to wake up and have to do something, it takes me about two hours to care for the birds, the wholesalers are delivering food, I get a box of mealworms flown in from Chicago once a month, I go to the market and buy everything they need, I spend a fortune at the Korean's. I like them to eat early in the morning, I give them filtered water. It's kind of like taking care of children. It's a nice way to start the day. Of course, there are days when I'd rather they weren't here.

They eat a lot of protein. A lot of people think birds just eat seeds. They need a lot of protein; a lot of birds will suffer later in life from only eating seeds.

The birds have a sense that this is their house. They don't like the lights on past nine o'clock, they'll scream. Although they do like parties. They like it when people come over. One loves to be on TV. There is a social aspect to them, but they need to be secure. They need to know they're going to get food at the same time every day, that horrible things aren't going to happen to them. They like the cleaning girl.

One hates women. He'll get down on the floor and spy the one open spot on a woman's shoe and bite really badly.

They figure stuff out. The sounds they make are incredible. It's a thrill to hear them. I've had a few unfortunate ones. Like this Indian water hen that I had, he would crow all night long, loudly. I thought I was going to lose my mind. It turned out this friend of mine had a mate for him, and he's up there now, and he's stopped doing it. He was crying for a mate.

I've been saving all their feathers. I'm interested in doing a feather-lined room.

All the birds can handle extreme cold, strangely enough, when the heat goes off.

My African gray parrots were both born in captivity, one in Arizona, one in Massachusetts. They're supposed to be the smartest and best talkers of all the birds. One of them talks a lot, the other one doesn't say much. But he learns things very quickly. It's more than mimicry—they have this sense of when to say things, they remember people's names. There's one cleaning person named Debby, she hadn't been here for a long time, and he hadn't used her name, and she came in and he said "Debby," after two years of not seeing this person.

They do one thing that really annoys me. They mimic the ring of the telephone. And I really can't tell the difference. They're very good at imitating mechanical noises. It's getting to be a problem. They call the cat, they tell the other birds to shut up. They're very smart. I've heard of parrots who've learned whole operas. I don't work very hard at teaching them anything. They just pick things up.

I was painting saints with animals around them, and then started to leave the saints out. I've been using birds in my work from day one. The cage thing happened very spontaneously; it's about the layering of the wire, and to me it's a metaphor. The bird is always the symbol of the soul in Christianity, and in *The Egyptian Book of the Dead,* and the cage represents the body. There's a Hindu legend about a tiger with a birdcage on its head. It's about the soul in the house, and how the body is a temporary thing. It's also about urban light, how these forms come in: it's never dark in the city. I have twenty-seven windows, so there's always these traffic lights, car lights, sirens, all these light forms coming through. I'm addressing that, and the survival of some things outside the jungle. You know, people are always saying, "I want to take my bird back to the jungle and let him loose." Well, why don't they go back to the jungle themselves? Animals don't know how to take care of themselves if they've been born and bred in captivity.

The grid motif, the wire mesh thing, meant a lot to me. It took me a long time to arrive at it in my painting even though I'd been living around it for such a long time. Somebody mentioned that my paintings have a lot to do with Cornell, and I'd forgotten how much wire mesh there is in his work—I remember in his show at the Modern, there was a whole room of bird boxes.

One of my favorite things is the Boccioni painting *The City Rises*, that light coming through. How does it all function? There has to be a God, there's no way that all this wouldn't self-destruct immediately if there wasn't some divine plan. With the birds, even, anything could happen, absolutely anything, and somehow it all functions, they live and get fed.

A lot of these animals would be extinct in nature, and are surviving through symbiosis with human beings. There's one catch to all that, however: the gene pool; you need new genes, you can't keep breeding the same things. They're doing all these computerized tests, and eventually—well, time's up. But it's prolonging the inevitable, unless they come up with some cloning thing. Some guy in Florida was breeding these black cockatoos, he got about ninety-five of them. He just died, and left a lot of money to keep it all going. But at some point they've got to get new genes in there. I'm not a breeder in any sense of the word. I lend my birds out to be bred.

They have very few medical problems. I have a good friend who's a vet, she comes here and helps me. A lot of times, animals heal themselves. I believe your time of death is fixed at your time of birth, it's a Hindu belief; the way you die is only in keeping with the way you live. I've had a couple of miraculous recoveries and a number of deaths that were unexplainable. But relatively speaking, everybody's in pretty good shape.

PATTI SMITH

Mirza

MY GRANDFATHER WAS the village potter. He was also the keeper of a famous stream. It was said to have curative powers, and people came from great distances to fill tiny bottles to wear around their necks. All about were trees. The willow curving above the tiled roof of my grandfather's house. The cypress heading the garden at stream's end and just beyond, past the workshed, the dense blossoming of his orchard. In summer the blossoms fell, carpeting the earth. In autumn the golden fruit followed, fragrant and sweet. The people, having filled their bottles, would buy the fruit and my grandfather's wares. His bowls were especially prized. All of his love fused in their uncommon glaze. Each imperishable, unique.

On the eve of my fourteenth year, he sent a messenger with gifts and a letter requesting that I come and serve as his apprentice. I would learn all that he knew and one day inherit his land and continue his work. My father agreed, and the next morning, as my mother wept, I packed my sack, called my dogs, and said my farewells. It was a long way and the messenger and I returned on foot, in silence. My dogs ran on ahead in chase of a hare. As we approached the familiar stream I too broke into a run. The evening's last light heightened the beauty of the woodland, the orchards and the surrounding hills, and I could not contain my joy. I arrived at my grandfather's door flushed and road weary. He welcomed me with a bowl of warm milk and thick sour bread. I could not help thinking that soon I would be drinking from my own bowl turned by my own hand.

That night my dreams were invaded by the baying of my dogs. I dreamed of the forest, the stream and sky. I dreamed everywhere I ran the earth was my own. The next morning I began my studies. I worked hard. The days bled into seasons. I was happy there. My dogs ran free and I was experiencing new sensations, the most consuming being the power I felt when I threw at the wheel.

The seasons bled into years. My grandfather spent a lot of time in space. He would sit for hours in the garden and stare until something in his line of vision would disintegrate, break into a thousand tiny flashes and just disappear. I watched his progress from a small opening in the potter's shed. A rock, a bush, and then, to my great horror, his favorite dog. After that he stayed in the garden all of the time—even at night.

One morning I sat before him and our eyes locked. Remembering the dog, I held on. His eyes were like violet flowers—centuries of love and death seemed to swirl in their purple depths. Mine were white—untested, pure. Our energies met full force, but I was younger and stronger and he collapsed. After that I avoided his eyes. I kept my dogs penned in a nearby field, and in a corner of the shed I nursed Mirza, an orphaned whelp, the only surviving trace of my grandfather's favorite dog.

I loved my grandfather but I loved my life more. I spent a

lot of time in the hills with Mirza, searching the caves for new deposits of clay. Soon I would be a man, I would have my own kiln, be my own master. My grandfather remained in the garden, an almost discarnate fixture. I continued my work.

On the morning of my eighteenth year I extracted a special bowl from the kiln. I delighted as always in the birth process of my wares. A firebox provided the heat which passed up through the firebars into the pottery chamber, the chamber of clay dying with the solid birth of the object. Demolishing the temporary structure, I scraped away the dead clay and turned the bowl in my hands—a gift for Mirza. Destruction and creation commingling in a single piece. Something welled up inside me as I placed the bowl before Mirza, and her eyes, violet and wide, seemed to tell me it was good.

That same evening, my grandfather vanished. The people of the village gathered with their torches and searched the field and forest. They never found him. It was my opinion, though I told no one but Mirza, that he had turned his gaze inward and consumed himself. I formed an urn in his memory and applied a special glaze, an almost unholy shade of purple, to match my grandfather's eyes. I set it in the garden where he once sat. I noticed visitors averted their eyes when passing it.

All that had been my grandfather's came into my hands. And I reached beyond him, extending into sculpture. I formed cherubs, statues, monoliths. My fame grew; my wealth increased. Life was good. I was strong and healthy. I could have my pick of the village girls. Yet I dwelled on the outskirts of my own prosperity. I preferred to be alone with Mirza and my new dog, a wolf cub I found in a cave while

searching for clay. In time he became my constant companion. Mirza would lie by the urn, regarding us with a mixture
of sadness and reproach. But I was too restless to comfort
her. I let her draw comfort from the peace of the garden
while I went hunting with my wolf dog.

The village widows, bred on superstition, warned me
against him. He was a wolf, an agent of evil. I only laughed.
He was but myself—a loner with an unapologetic, lively nature. He reveled in his solitude, as did I. At day's end, when
the last of the light highlighted all the beauty that was now
mine, I stood and surveyed it with greedy pleasure. I opened
the store of wine; I drank with abandon. Within me was a
burning. "I am my own kiln," I cried. I conjured waves of
light, arms, torsos that became infamous mold in my hands.
I danced upon the low wood tables as my beast howled. It
was our joy.

On brilliant nights we emerged from the shed to dance
in the moonlight, only to find Mirza hovering over our joy
like an old Greek nurse. She was like the women in the village and I took to treating her as I treated them, with con-
tempt. Perhaps my wolf felt this from me, because he too was
showing signs of hostility toward her.

Mirza, who I had rescued with such care from my grandfather's gaze. Who I had fed from a bottle, brushed, and ca-
ressed. Who I had whispered all my youthful hopes and desires. But I was no longer a youth, but a man. And she no
longer a pup, but a stinging grandmother.

Every race is conquering. She was killed by my wolf dog.
She already belonged to the past, sympathetic, beyond dignity. She was lying there under the cypress tree pouring

syrup from her clock. The spring in the back of her neck was clear and sweet. I don't know. I never drank from it. Nor did I pass long in those eyes, as necessary as the glasses for a 3-D movie. She was sympathetic. In the remote soil of her eyes were the ruins, the arcades, the archways of history.

The women beat my wolf. They demanded his skin but I could not kill him. He was more myself than dog. That idiot smile. He cowered when he saw me but bared his teeth. In a rage I cut them, humiliating him. I penned him up. I put him out to run with the old women. The women with rattles in their chests. I no longer went out to hunt. I longed to run with him, share his humiliation. Maybe I loved him more than before. I grew weak. The lore of fathers. I watched him, lying beneath the cypress tree. When the sky was heavy with almonds. When the sun beat down. When the fanwise invasion of wind whistles in the mouth. He lies there. His eyes, that were white and burning, now remote and sympathetic; resting directly on the future with the sticky sweetness of a clock.

Several nights after I had filed the teeth of my wolf I noticed the atmosphere shifting around me. I seemed to identify with everything. I was the foundation, the sticky coil of a vase. I was odorless stacks of fresh-fired plates, the cold stone of the kiln. It was impossible to work. Rolling the coils was the worst. They became alive in my hand. The lovely unrelenting statues would undulate in smoke. The freshly molded huntress waved her wrists, and I could discern her hips rotating sweetly beneath her girdle of soft wet clay. With a rope and pulley I laid her against the wall.

I was sweating and shivering and she was beckoning. I

pressed my lips against her melting face, the coils of her hair squishing between my eager fingertips. I became addicted to a paste of almond meal and paregoric, of humping and shattering art. My trade suffered. Tourists and holy men sought vessels—souvenirs of the graced grounds where my dogs ran in packs. I suffered, passing for hours on a bed of dust, tormented with lust for objects, walls, and an intense craving for a sweet and sticky gas to blot me out. The dogs were wilder than ever. I couldn't breathe. The women had a special tea sent to me.

Then a new shift. The sensation of invasion by a palpitating fist of warm light. The tea was sweet. At the bottom of the glass was a colorless grape. In a few hours it turned. I put it in the glazed bowl I had made for Mirza. It suddenly dominated the room. It was a breast with a sore and poking nipple, the oiled bottom of a slave. I lay on my stomach, my heart pounding against the stone floor—my sex obliterated by objects—the bowl grew still larger. The vibrating grape split and revealed a white snake. Someone had eaten a portion of it. Something was alive and wriggling inside of me. My belly swelled like the cheeks of a glass-blower. I couldn't move. The pain increased into the sound of wailing curses. The women entered, circled, and shook their rattles. Montage of trees, bowl, and canine teeth. Who would feed my wolf . . .

The sting of relief won out.

I lay there conscious only of the motion of my head rising, of lips to a glass or a stream of powder entering my vein. When at last the fever subsided I rose with a start. I dressed in a simple suit of cloth stuff and inspected everything. The statues and vessels had been preserved with wet sheets.

Nothing lost. Everything was blooming, the air vibrant and sweet.

I found my wolf dog lying in the garden. Perhaps he had shared my fever as he had once shared my joy. But no one had cared for him and he was hardly more than a shadow, a translucent coat of fur stretched beneath the cypress tree. I called for a boy to fetch a syphon and the bowl that had once belonged to Mirza. I remembered the spring and drew from it. I had never drunk from it but the waters were legendary. I dipped from them and poured between his filed teeth. I felt woozy. I laid my head upon the coat of my wolf dog and slept.

Idiot rule. The big tree fucks the small grass. Tomorrow I am a tadpole, an insignificant shell. But this afternoon I pass for a long time dreaming and feeling a thrill to the kill of Mirza. To a time when my young wolf dog was mad with the projection of the human personality.

SUSAN SWAN

Insect Love

AHEAD ON THE Great Sound a yacht is moving slowly west to the horizon, where the rock humps of the Watchers lie like fallen Indian gods in the water. The yacht inches toward a cluster of sailboats that billow and flutter like white cabbage butterflies on a plate of fresh water. You see only bare backs and the dark balls of heads sitting on shoulders, but I am waiting for you in that clump of bodies. Your yacht pulls aside mine. You climb noiselessly up the swimming ladder, pad slowly over in your canvas sneakers, and discover me lying on the floor of the yacht offering up my body to you like a prayer.

Near me a slender man stands holding a film camera. I am uncertain of my beauty, but in the lens of his camera I float like a golden-limbed summer creature with masses of long hair as yellow as sand, and eyes that shine like July skies.

I beckon with an oil-creamed arm and you lie down beside me. Good. You are succumbing. I want you to stay lost with me in this void of pleasure where we can be as single-minded as insects and not admit that time is creeping by us bit by bit out here in the open, inching in its eternal way like the yacht moving toward the billowing sails of the lasers. At this moment, you are not X years old, you are only X summers old.

Bewildered, you look up at the two bodies swaying above us. The slender man is my lover, Child Cape. His face under branches of feathery hair makes you think of Struwwelpeter, the naughty boy in the German children's story who was beaten with a birch rod. The third character, Bobby, is the pregnant woman in a bikini. She stands at the wheel of the yacht. You take in the light pink lipstick smeared on the sulky, pouty mouth, the tanned honey-brown skin, the hanks of platinum hair foaming out from under a floppy canvas hat.

Isn't it shocking the way her stomach surges over the triangle of her bikini like an astonished chocolate face? The belly button sticking out in a point is the nose. The orange V of the bikini bottom is the mouth. The two circles of cloth on the breasts, puffy orange eyes. You are a little startled at how virginal I seem next to Bobby, who looks like a vixen in a B movie. You gawk at her breasts shaped like plump zucchinis and her tanned globular belly.

Bobby bespeaks activity behind closed doors while I project innocence. Go on. Don't stop. Compare Bobby and me, body part by body part. We are all objects who come in different shapes and sizes. And I take pride in the part of my being that is pure objectness. My wrists and ankles are as slim as the forelegs of a deer. I have no stretch marks but I have borne no children. And my breasts are as small as a boy's. That's a strike against me. I am also slightly horse-faced with big, sincere eyes. My left eye is a shade more blue than my right. That's another defect. Still, I have a good face as faces go. Sometimes I forget that I have become what is considered good looking. At twenty-four, I still think of myself as a sexual loser.

This is also me to the extent that I can know myself: intense, disarmingly candid, a novelist with a hesitant speaking manner that doesn't hide a nature inclined toward dichotomies. There is I the iconoclast who never wants to hurt anyone's feelings, and I the doer and I the dreamer. Not to mention I the theoretician or I the lotus-eater and I the Puritan—and, of course, I the truth-teller and I the liar.

And this is Bobby: moody, generous, a maverick who seeks the setting of a conformist to express herself. Bobby had a shotgun marriage at nineteen but she still thinks of herself as a sexual winner despite the role of matron she plays in her family. Her lover is Jonah Prince, whose island lies in the middle of the Great Sound, to the north of the Watchers.

The heat is baking out here on the open water. Our procession chugs slowly away from the fluttering sails of the lasers and the mysterious shaggy pines growing right down to the edge of the islands, their roots sunk deep into slabs of rocks that volcanoes left behind millions of years ago. The sunlight this far out is an ugly mauve red on the backs of my eyelids. I open my eyes and look at Bobby. Why hadn't I noticed before? Bobby is metamorphosing in the white watery heat as we head toward Jonah's island. She turns her node-shaped head my way, her mandibles quivering, and I see for the first time the August light shining in her compound eyes. Then my fecund ant queen fixes her gaze with the stupidity of instinct on Jonah Prince's untreed dome of granite. She scratches her thorax and imagines the colony she will found there with her new ant husband away from the mess of her old burrow. In their new royal apartment, she and Jonah will hold a mating party that's never over while an endless procession of chitinous slaves crawl around her mountainous abdomen. From that swollen bulb—thirty thousand times larger than my body—Bobby's eggs will spurt like white pudding—one in every ten minutes. Then Child, her favorite worker, will carry off the newborn egg and deposit it with the other eggs in the hundreds of cavities Child and others like him have chewed in the walls of Bobby's new home. And Bobby will lie still and let her ant workers regurgitate my honeydew into her open mouth.

Yes, I am metamorphosing too. I am round and green—Child's favorite color. I am an aphid. I have almost no head, only two tiny, dark eyes like black buttons. My mouth is a beak, a sweet little sucking spear I use for piercing plant tissues. Child's mouth is at my anus. He licks me until I drip helplessly with the sweaty honey he likes.

I could flick the drops away with my hind leg but there is no need to do anything. It's Child's job to dispose of my fluids. In the summer he carries me from plant to plant for my feedings, and when winter comes he will take my aphid babies down into Bobby's new ant burrow.

"Now's our chance," is the pheromone message Child passes to me on his spongy tongue. Then in a little show of manly pleasure, my beloved rears up on his hindquarters, his forelegs twitching like he couldn't be happier. I tremble slightly as the dark tube of his thorax eclipses the sun . . . huge, fierce—Child is like a god to me, our insect father Protoptera . . . the beginning of bug life. You see, Child has wings and I don't—generations of herd life have caused them to wither. I am absolutely helpless without the care of my keeper.

Eagerly now, Child drops back to the ground and lets his antennae graze my skin until I begin to leak with moisture, the way I am wont to do. Slowly my love sap drips onto his mandibles until they start to shine with the colors of the rainbow . . . Child is milking me, his dark bug eyes soft with love and I sit back on my slender legs, push my drooling anus into his mouthpart.

And suddenly Child's antennae stop waving. His head snaps back. Child hears a puff of noise. I hear it too. A sound like feathers fanning the air. Then I see your murderous shape towering over us—winged, pop-eyed and snake-snouted. You, too, have metamorphosed. You are a praying mantis straddling the slippery deck, your hideous triple-jointed forearms waving eerily with the rocking motion of the boat.

Child and I stare in terror at your murderous face. The puffing noise is coming from the transparent veined wings spreading like sails on either side of your terrible head. Yes, your head is terrible—two intent little black eyes stare at me fixedly beneath long antennae that curve to the sky like a set of horns.

Once upon a time I used to think of you as an imaginary friend, but the proper term for you is reader. Of course, you are as protean as we are. You have a body and your own sensations and you too can change shape at will. Would I be so insensitive to consign you to a narrow psychological reality? You are my ally and necessary witness.

If only you weren't a praying mantis. Why can't you be a bug with a nicer disposition? How about the common house-

fly—*Fannia canicularis*, for example. The one that doesn't
bite and flies tirelessly around light fixtures and human
heads, driving everyone to distraction. Or maybe you'd prefer
to be a heat bug with the little ruby telescopes that explore the
air over their heads and the huge, multifaceted eyes that make
them look slightly paranoid. It's their abdominal plates that
make the happy drumming sound we hear each summer.
After all, this is the year of the cicada. Hundreds of them are
emerging from the ground as we speak—shedding their old
skins like car wrecks on the granite islands of the Sound. In
the southern United States, cicada grubs live underground
for thirteen years. Here they remain seventeen years in the
dark. Which is why Canadian cicadas love heat and sunshine
more than cicadas from New Orleans.

You don't appear to be listening. In fact, something bar-
barous has happened while I wasn't looking. How else did
Bobby get lifted off the ground? And now she's in your spike-
studded grip, her poor head swinging from side to side in
alarm. I scream, "Don't you dare!" but no sound comes out
of my mouth. I hear a gruesome crunch and all at once
Bobby's eggs burst out of her like foam and spray your face
until your little bulbous eyes are covered with her babies. My
queen's panoply of legs jerks pitifully then stops flailing.
Bobby's abdomen is gone and half her thorax is missing.
Now you fasten those eyes of yours on Child. Oh, please—
not him! Let Child be so his antennae can keep stroking my
lovesick abdomen.

I should have known you'd pay no attention. We are all
insects here, driven by our natures. Behind me I hear your
grisly handiwork—the little snaps and pops as Child's hindquarters crack open. I will be eaten too but I can't make a

move to save myself! Child's strokes grow weaker. Once, twice more, he bumps my anus, and I flow on like the waters of the Great Sound, like a river, milky as a cow only good for dairying, I must hold still and let whoever has need feed on me.

The Frog Prints

T HIS IS A TALE of Chelsea. Of Old Chelsea, as the brochures call it, which has low Georgian houses, and wrought-iron balconies, and acacia trees in paved gardens, and rooms with silky walls and tasselled curtains; and the other Chelsea, where the slum buildings in the abandoned streets are boarded up, and the tops of the shops look jagged, as if they had been sawn off to meet the grey sky that comes in off the river, and men and girls with eyes like rats' eyes hunt together in packs. Our heroine, Griselda, came from one and was irresistibly attracted to the other. Her name was Greaves—the same as the painter Greaves, who lived in the shadow of Whistler but devoted his life to the most exquisite pink and yellow and grey water-colours of the river, of the masts of boats, and the tramp steamers that gave out little puffs of black smoke like a cigarette bought in a joke shop. Some of these pictures hung in Griselda Greaves' parents' home. So wherever she turned—to the bow window above the wrought-iron balcony, which looked straight down a neat street to the Embankment—or to the mirror which hung high on the stairs and reflected the stretch of water Turner had seen from his parapet, or to the framed aquatints on the walls—all that ever met her eye was an expanse of water. Sometimes, when the tide was very low, the houseboats at the end of the street lay in black, evil-smelling mud. Greaves had painted this too; broken wooden staves, remnants of an ancient jetty, poking up out of the thickest black Indian ink. But it didn't take long for the river to fill up again—and for the greys, the delicate water greys after which Griselda was named, to take possession, to fill the mind's eye, both inside the house and out.

Griselda Greaves was the only daughter of a fussy, affected father and a rich mother with a Mr Punch chin. She had a strong sense of grievance, perhaps because she had been forced to take a name that spelt sorrow, a name she had never wanted anyway. Her mother's parents had been delighted with Mr Greaves, and had found him cultivated, and she had been married off to him when she was eighteen, many years ago. But because of this, Mrs Greaves was determined her daughter should find true love when it came. And this contrasted strongly with the views of Mr Greaves, who had learnt from his own fairly comfortable experience that it was possible in the end to come to love anyone. Between them, these contradictory parents had brought Griselda up to see herself as a rare and precious jewel, and it seemed unlikely that she would ever find time to love anyone other than herself. What they had neglected, in simple absent-mindedness, to provide on this path to permanent immaturity, the late twentieth century amply made up for. When Griselda was born, the Age of Adolescence had already been under way for nearly two generations. The first focussing of her limpid grey eyes was on a world consisting of adults in blue jeans and beards, long hair and more denim again, and guitars like toys strapped to their chests. The first music she heard, beyond the gracious Mozart of her mother's drawing-room and the silences of John Cage that emanated from the other Georgian houses, was the plangent wail of country and western, the metallic thump, like a hundred giant super-market baskets being dragged across the heavens, of the lat-est acid rock. And from her earliest days, concealed behind the covers of the compulsory Struwwelpeter, she read head comics until her eyes ran.

It was Griselda's father in particular who tried daily to drag her into his own past. (He had come from an interna-tional 'artistic' family, Florence, Austria, palazzos, and uncles who had sternly painted fat and juicy women in the nude—they were all impoverished now.) But he failed to return Griselda to a world she had never known, where the iced cakes, and long platonic friendships, and piano concerts held at the feet of none other than the great Michelangelo's David, summed up perfection for him. He hoped, when the time came, that a young man like the young men these uncles had been, would be the one to woo his daughter. If, in the long-dead world of the Greaves', love and virtue and courage were still words emblazoned in gold over their pri-vate box at the opera, in the world to which Griselda was in-troduced, and in which the pretty eighteenth-century houses sat so uneasily by the timeless riverside: these words had never been spoken or heard. In their different ways, the Greaves parents hoped for a happy future for their only daughter, though it would be difficult to know how they en-visaged it. Luckily, love is blind.

So here we have Griselda, surrounded by water on all sides, grey-eyed and inward-turned—and here we have her on a February morning, when it's cold as steel in the streets, and warm and snug in the bow-windowed drawing room, where there hangs a chandelier of artificial rain and the walls are as grey-washed with clouds as her eyes. Griselda is champing with impatience. There is nothing for her to do! She went to a ball last night, given by a pretentious friend of her mother's called Jacintha de Last. The young men bored her. She wants to go to her real friends, in the other Chelsea, but her mother is watching her carefully. Substances, or shadows of substances, have been found clinging to Griselda—on her clothes, in her hair the colour of ash, the sweet snowy breath of drugs. Mrs Greaves has alerted Mr Greaves. Both are speechless with shock. And both are acting themselves as naturally as possible—which has of course made Griselda suspicious as well as impatient. It's as if the drugs had entered the veins of her parents, and subtly altered their personality, through over-emphasis: Mr Greaves has put on a thick slug of a green cravat to stress his old 'artiness', his ability to understand absinthe or hashish. Mrs Greaves has been in her sable-lined mackintosh all day, shifting Meissen figurines from the cellar to the study, and back again. Griselda looks out at an unending afternoon over the river, and her teeth are clenched.

—Griselda, shall we make a plan to go to the Courbet Exhibition? Mr Greaves sings out from his 'den'.

Mr Greaves' den is off the drawing room, through a door that looks wide enough only for a dog. There is a smell of toast always in there, and of yellowing paper, from the magazine *Asterisk* which Mr Greaves used to edit when he was young. Griselda shudders. She looks round in obvious distaste at the ageing Bohemian, thick-waisted in a silk dressing gown, who stands pathetically confronting her.

Enter Mrs Greaves with a Chelsea dove, so beautiful, so white, so priceless, in her arms.

—I do love him, Griselda, don't you? But I think it would be interesting to get another valuation from Sothebys!

So Griselda considers her parents' ideas of love: the one, an eternal trudge around a museum, a 'coming to see the point of' yet another obscure artist; the other, in agonies of adulation for an object, always imagining that it can be sold and exchanged for the 'real thing', the final object beyond worth. Griselda's lips curl.

—I want some money to go shopping for new clothes, she says.

—But that's all you'll be doing? both Greaves' burst out too soon and together, their cover blown, their anxiety as idiotic on their faces as the gape of an actor who has muffed his lines.

—Of course that's all I'll be doing!

Mrs Greaves burrows in her crocodile bag. Now that Griselda is so much at an advantage, now her parents have made such fools of themselves, she must at all costs be humoured. She pulls out a sheaf of twenty-pound notes.

—Here you are, darling. I hope you find something nice!

And Griselda sets off, shrugging away the neat hallway with the fanlight and the riverscapes, and goes out into the wintry Christmas card street, and walks as fast as she can to the King's Road. She will keep her word in one sense. There's a necklace she wants, of jet beads, polished up as bright as cats' eyes, which is labelled 'Devil's Tears' in the window of the Purple Emporium, and which would look as wicked and degenerate as the mist coming off a witch's cauldron when worn with her habitual grey rags. She will drop in there, and buy it. She can imagine the cool stare of approval from her real friends when she turns up in it at the shop past the bend in the road. For Griselda takes her image seriously. In the summer she walks the King's Road bare foot. Her rags are palest chiffon and torn twenties' silks: she is sometimes known as Cinders, or the Match Girl. And with any luck, there will be ear-rings of jet to go with it; rivulets of sparkling black to go down the side of her white face and ashy hair.

The Purple Emporium is in that part of the King's Road which has still a tatty smartness. There are two floors to the building, and a roof garden where the hippy tourists eat jam buns and look down at the punks in summer. Griselda stops at the display window, and stares in at the kimonos, and half-broken miniature tin cars, and ivory prayer books with the pages ripped out. But the jet necklace isn't there! Someone has been quicker—for once. Now, in its place, is a mandrake root, with a spidery writing on the label beneath, simply saying 'Mandragore'. There is a nasty bottle, in which something is preserved in ancient spirit: an adder, perhaps, or a no-longer-edible ginseng root. And there is a print—Griselda's eyes are averted at once, prints remind her of her father—of what seems to be a maiden drawing water at a well.

Griselda decides to buy the mandrake root. It may cause something of a stir. Or they might grind it up like rhinoceros horn. She goes in to the emporium, and looks arrogantly across the counter at the girl, gypsy-scarfed, who runs the stall. The girl knows her, and she knows the girl, but they have never exchanged a civil word.

—I'll have the mandragore, says Griselda. How much is it?

—It's not for sale, says the girl.

—Oh! says Griselda—and suddenly she wants the mandrake root more than anything she has ever wanted in her life—more than life itself. The jet necklace recedes into the distance, banal and undesirable as the spangled ball dress Griselda wore last night to go to the tedious ball. The root grows in her mind and soon blocks everything else: white, twisted as a tree-fungus, phallic, menacing, one-eyed. She reaches out to touch it where it lies on the worn velvet cloth beside the print. And the last thing she sees is the girl stallholder's eyes, alive with malicious laughter under a Byzantine fringe of gold sequins hanging from her gypsy scarf.

The print in the window of the Purple Emporium was nineteenth century, of an early sixteenth-century Scottish scene. 'A girl drawing water from the Well at the World's End,' said the spidery writing under it. And, 'From a Complaynt of Scotland.' Inexpert hands had washed in the greys of the desolate scene, where a single hawthorn tree, forked, split by lightning, stood to the side of the stone well. The ground was grey too, as if the grass had withered. The girl was richly dressed, and knelt with what at first appeared to be a mandolin, but on closer inspection turned out to be a sieve. Not surprisingly, her expression was desperate. She was trying to draw water with the sieve. Something about her small, Scotch face was determined, though: she had been brought up, it seemed, to get what she wanted to get.

The only smudge—or it looked like a smudge in the otherwise careful and sparse print—was to the side of the well where the girl was kneeling. It was directly under her face, and like many inkblots had a strangely identifiable, almost animate quality. It seemed to be staring up at her, appealing

to her—and it looked remarkably like a frog, or perhaps a
toad, with head cocked to one side and eyes protruding from
the blot as if the clumsy artist had had a hair entangled in his
nib and had tried to banish it with a pounce that had turned
into a smudge. Certainly the frog was the strongest and
blackest element in the picture, and the girl seemed to be in a
hypnotized relation to it: it was so placed, centrally, that
whichever way she turned she would be bound to be drawn
back into its orbit again.

Griselda walked up the King's Road towards the bend.
She had the air of someone walking in a trance—but then so
did most of the strolling population there, whether the air
was put on to impress the locals and would be quickly removed in another part of London, or whether true hallu-
cinogenics had been taken. It was a Friday afternoon and
there was a good mixture of punks, Teds, middle-aged hippies, bright young Chelsea housewives, hip publishers and
wholefood manufacturers in braided velvet and boiler suits.
Coveys of gays went in and out of the launderette on the dramatic corner, the S-bend of the King's Road. Two girls in
brightly dyed feather boas made a twitter around Griselda as
she went—they knew her but it was clear she couldn't recognize them. From a Baghdad restaurant, beyond the treacle
cakes and the exhausted flies crawling in glass cases, the low
sticky tables inlaid with mother of pearl, the tasselled curtains of old clothes, a young androgyne, a friend of Griselda's
shouted a greeting. But she walked on. Her eyes were as grey
as the February sky. Her beautiful, ragged, grey Persian lamb
coat hung from her shoulders as if her body had grown suddenly smaller inside it. Her grey suede boots, which but-
toned up the sides, stepped neatly over the cracked pave-

ments like the fetlocks of an overbred horse. People started
to nudge each other as she wandered across the road, oblivious to traffic. There goes the Grey Lady. Whatever's that she's
got with her today? That's Griselda Greaves.

Griselda was carrying the mandrake root. It was tucked
in her sleeve, like a miniature dog, with one gnarled end
sticking out. The expression on her face was rapt, but determined. She reached the bend in the road, looked back once
at the famous Chelsea mile, the gimcrack boutiques, the *trat-
torie*, the jeans bunched together like on racks like platoons
of decapitated sailors, the Town Hall, queen cake of the neo-
classical—and plunged ahead, following the swirl of the
pavement, to the last stretch before the World's End.

Immediately, as she rounded the corner, the crowds
thinned out and the real battle of the two Chelseas showed
itself. Griselda, unmoved, walked on.

The well was just opposite the pub at the World's End. To
the south of it, lay the yellow brick council flats with their
'adventure' compounds and open staircases like ramps in an
overground carpark. To the west were the boarded streets,
where Griselda headed, of houses ripe for demolition, and
warehouses of old PX clothes that the punks wore, and little
shops, spicy as India, where you could spend hundreds on an
outfit and get the white powder measured out to you at the
same time, in an unlit hole at the back. To the north, the
houses simply got smaller, until they looked like rows of
sheds under a wide sky. And to the east was the river, which
sent mists and gas-smog from the power station, always a
smell, thick and sweet and unnameable from the huge chim-
neys on the other side. The well was planted in the direct
centre of all this. A black hawthorn stood behind it. Griselda

paused as she drew near to the well, but she had clearly made up her mind as to her first destination. She laid the man-drake root carefully on the well's edge, by the sieve which was awaiting her there, and walked west, into the street most shuttered with faded, splitting plywood against the outside world. No one here seemed to pay the slightest attention to her. She might have been a ghost, grey as the air she walked in. No one paid any attention to the well, either, or the scorched, broken hawthorn. But this may have been because there was a particularly wide section of pavement outside the pub at the World's End, and the residents were used to things being introduced by the council: cherry trees most often but sometimes odd pieces of modern sculpture, to which category the well and the tree might conceivably belong.

Cutting in strips and sniffing, Griselda and her friends huddle in a ruined room. Her friends are called: Night Nurse, Food Halls, Watford Gap, Fire Down Below and Airport Lounge. How different they are from Jacintha de Last, whose boring party Griselda was made to suffer through last night! They have spiked hair and boots as nailed as a caveman's club in a strip cartoon. Their eyes have been painted round with water-lily leaves of black. After the first parrot-house of greetings, and fondling of the mandrake root, they are all busily cutting the cocaine on a long Paris 1920s mirror with a gold sunburst at the top which Airport Lounge stole from the shop of a gay antiquary at the far end of the King's Road. Griselda's ragged grey fur, and her soft suede legs like a smoky cat's, settle down on the dust of the floorboards. And she takes the brown twenty-pound notes her mother gave her from her python bag the colour of a desert stone. They sniff the white powder through the notes. They start to see the meaning, the terrible clarity, of the long chinks in the wood that boards up the windows. The chinks are white windows, diamond white, into the void. The bright February whiteness comes in on them there in algebraic formulae, the world outside cracks into a mosaic. The eyes grow brighter, the nostrils numb.

After a while, still holding the root, Griselda wanders to the makeshift door, crawls under a plank and takes the squatter's exit into the street. Everything is as quiet as before, as if the meaning of the world hadn't just been seen under the low roof behind her. The streets, having avoided conversion from the squat decency of lower-middle-class Victorian homes to the waste of concrete, the shuddering staked-out laburnum, the eyeless towers, have a resigned and muffled air. There are some people still allowed to be living in the houses, and they pass Griselda without so much as a look. Some are women pushing baskets on wheels, others are pushing children. Sometimes one of 'them' like Griselda, blows their way, but if these women show anything it's no more than a twitch of the shoulders at a scrap of waste paper, a floating piece of transparent rubbish in the wind. Griselda and her friends simply don't exist: and it's quite right, they don't, for they are living in a different area of space.

Griselda wanders to the well. A pale sun comes out for a moment through the thick white clouds over World's End. The sieve is just where it was—to pick it up is to feel the frailness of the wood and the holes of the sieve are like the pencil strokes, the cross-hatchings of a drawing. Griselda takes it up. Her face is as pale as Ingres paper. For a while she sits on the edge of the well and dips in the sieve, watching water that is black and gives back no reflection, hardly ripples at the touch of the sieve. Then she tires, and there is something tiring, frustrating about the inability of the sieve to retain the water, even for a second—and she sits on the paving by the well and begins to go through her bag for treasures. For everything looks different now, and is invested with the meaning normally denied in everyday life: her keys become her toys, her bright round little mirror in her compact a glass star which she can revolve slowly in the palm of her hand. Soon she is kneading the brown twenty-pound notes into a ball, and throwing it in the air. Still the stolid shoppers pass her by, as the natives do hippies in their hill kingdoms. One look at the girl's face, haggard and ashen, the cendré hair which is now like the grey locks round an old woman's face, the eyes desperate, staring upwards in their private vision, and no one wants to try to break through her silence, to take her to a hospital or to the police. She might shatter if she were dragged away, and become a part of the crazy paving where she sits.

So Griselda's ball of paper gold bobs in the air—and plop!—down it goes into the well. She pulls herself up disconsolately. For a moment, reality edges into her mind, but like an ill-fitting piece in a jigsaw, is rejected. Still—just for a moment—money, the money of Mrs Greaves' family, the money which makes it possible for Griselda to be there in her rags, and not in a Marks jumper and skirt behind the counter in a department store—that money which Night Nurse and Fire Down Below get when they sign on, and which buys the food they need between trips, appears concrete and important. The alchemy has been effected: magic and base metal, married in the spaces of Griselda's brain, give sudden value to the paper ball—and she almost tips into the well, trying to retrieve it.

The frog looks back up at Griselda. It is squatting on her ball, which makes a little globular raft. Its eyes are black and shiny—quite repulsive, Griselda thinks.

—You want this? says the frog. It paddles energetically with a webbed foot: Griselda shudders. The oily waters of the well are staining her money.

—You may certainly have it. And I shall come back to your home with you, continues the frog.

—But give it to me! says Griselda. She is leaning over so far now, and the sun has come through the clouds and is shining directly over her shoulder, that she sees her own distracted face in the water below, with the frog floating across her brow, like a black smudge. She groans. A family pass a few feet away from her, on the way back from Sainsburys, and there is a sudden sharp smell of cauliflower.

—Here I come! says Frog. And he jumps right out of the well, the paper ball gripped beneath him, like a child jumping on the big red balls that have small horns of rubber to hold on to. But the frog is cleverer than that—he has managed to bring the ball out by holding fast with his feet.

—Thank you, says Griselda faintly, when frog and ball land at her feet. Now if you don't mind, I'll take it home with me. Thank you again for all your help. (Griselda is losing her cocaine landscape quickly, and speaking like Mrs Greaves: her voice is distant, but full of authority). She bends down, but shrinks from actually detaching the frog from her money ball.

My love is like a root
It grows up through my mouth and chokes me
Cut it and it grows again
Right into your heart.

—What? cries poor Griselda when she realises this is the frog speaking. She seems overcome by nausea. And indeed, for the first time since she has been in the World's End, her presence is acknowledged by passers-by. She looks quite normal, though clearly in distress. The well and the hawthorn tree have disappeared. The frog and the ball of money aren't immediately visible, small as they are by Griselda's grey suede boot.

—If you can't like that kind of poetry I can try something else, says the frog—at the same time as a kindly woman is coming up to Griselda, parking her basket on wheels, and asking if she can help in any way.

—No—no thanks, says Griselda. While the frog begins:

Lady, ye'll ta'e me
To dwell on thy bosom
To sup at thy table
Thy fither and mither to call me their son.

No, no, cried Griselda, particularly repelled at the frog suddenly going into Scottish dialect, and remembering dimly, uncertainly, that the print in the Purple Emporium had been entitled 'A Complaynt for Scotland'. Where is she now? How dreadful if she should be somewhere in Edinburgh!

It looks to me as if we need an ambulance, says the kindly

woman, who is not deterred by Griselda's apparent rudeness to her. Come along my dear, sit on the bench here. And I'll hope the call box is working!

Lucky it is for Griselda and her new friend the frog that the callbox was vandalized weeks ago, and the woman gets quite immersed in there, jiggling for her lost coins. Griselda places the frog, the ball of money and the mandrake root on the sieve and goes as fast as her feet will carry her to the bend in the King's Road. Then she walks slowly home, swerved into sometimes by other people carrying strange objects for sale in the antique markets. Otherwise she is quite ignored. She arrives at her home exhausted, and runs up to the sitting-room—for when she is upset she likes to lie on the sofa there. Here father and mother are sitting either side of the fireplace. Mrs Greaves is reading a Sothebys catalogue and Mr Greaves is reading *The Portrait of a Lady.* When they see Griselda—see the state she's in, and see the frog and the repellent root too—all hell lets loose. But the Greaves are reasonable people, and soon they are offering Griselda a delicious meal. They even refrain from making a fuss when the frog sits by the side of her plate—in fact it's Griselda who is down-mouthed by its presence there, and sulkily complains that it's putting her off her food. The frog is good-natured, and nibbles away at her veal as if it had heard nothing at all. All the while the Greaves exchange worried and secret glances. What will they do when the night comes? It is already darkening, a February evening. Is Griselda under the influence of drugs? Will the frog go away?

Well, the answer to the first question lies in the imagination. A frog can live in air and water and Griselda was more water than air. As for the second and third these lead to a great many complications. We shall have to list a few of them here.

The three days which followed Griselda's return to the quiet street in Old Chelsea with the frog and the mandrake root were rendered unusual by both meteorological and pagan factors. It was mid-February—the worst storms for a half-century were battering the south-west coasts of England—and the Thames rose, grey-brown, solid as a wattle wall and invaded the street where the Greaves' lived. No sandbags would keep it out. It went in to the cellar, where it transformed the Chelsea doves and Meissen figures into muddy, prehensile lumps, the exquisite porcelain streaked with river filth. It went into the hall and the rest of the ground floor. But even Mr Greaves, with his developed aesthetic sense, refrained from mentioning how lovely the Greaves water-colours looked now they were hanging above their own element, reflecting, as it were, the original of the aquarelle. He went in galoshes into the library, and moaned at the despoliation of his big books of British birds. He went out once, but casting a worried look behind him as if he expected to find the whole house submerged on his return. It was true he returned in a better mood, with a parcel in brown paper under his arm. But by then the second day was well under way, and though he had noticed nothing, he found Mrs Greaves more hysterical than she had been when he had gone for his outing earlier in the morning. It wasn't just that her collection of priceless objects had turned into toads in the uninvited river—it was something else. Mrs Greaves had been to wake Griselda.

This second day was also the old pagan festival now known as St Valentine's. After a quiet evening the night before in which the Greaves had taken their daughter and the frog to a small French restaurant just outside the purlieus of Chelsea—and had suffered a good deal of embarrassment when a couple at the next table had ordered *grenouilles*—all four had retired to bed, the Greaves still determined to be friendly and not to antagonize Griselda, and Griselda allowing the frog up to her room with her usual show of bad temper. It was then, as St Valentine dawned, that Griselda learned of her deepest longings. She found herself, as the saying goes—she fell in love.

Frogs are not salacious animals. But they are slow and methodical. Griselda wept with pleasure when the cold-blooded beast sank down from its sleep on her breasts to the wet pond which awaited it below. She had never known herself to be so plentiful a source of water, a well where her new love could live forever. It was late when Griselda slept—and very hard to tell if frogs sleep at all.

By morning, though, it was sleeping quietly on the pillow next to Griselda. It waddled sideways again, and settled on Griselda's breast. Once there, it turned to the colour of her skin, like a chameleon, and as it nuzzled gently on her left nipple, making Griselda swoon with happiness in her half-sleep, it could have been mistaken for part of Griselda's own body.

By morning, Griselda was unrecognizable. She greeted her mother with a rapt smile, the frog by now coiled on her shoulder, its cold little head tucked under her ear. Mrs Greaves, who saw at once what had happened, ran away from the room and down the stairs in a panic. She ran without thinking into the brown water which still swirled at the foot of the banisters. She slipped, and screamed. It was here that

Mr Greaves found her, as he stepped into the sloppy hall with the square parcel under his arm.

—My dear, are you all right? (He helped her up; they went into the library. As Mrs Greaves had gone into the lower regions without galoshes it seemed madness to ruin the stair carpet by going back up in her present condition.)

—Griselda and that frog! gasped poor Mrs Greaves.

—It's only a passing fad, Mr Greaves assured her. He unwrapped the parcel and held his latest acquisition out in front of his wife. 'Look—isn't it fascinating? And to think I was just in the process of tracing the Greaves family back to Scotland! Well, here's the proof of it!'

Mrs Greaves stared dully at the print Mr Greaves had bought in the King's Road. 'What has complaynts for Scotland to do with the Greaves family?' she asked in a bitter tone. It seemed her husband and her daughter had both gone mad, for a smudge that was unmistakably a frog perched on the edge of a well in the print we have seen at work on the unfortunate Griselda. Were they both falling in love with frogs? Mrs Greaves thought in great despair. And when her roving gaze, going from the watercolours on the library walls to the hallway, began to take in the horrible truth, she could only let out a hoarse sob, cling to the desk for support, for it seemed hardly worth appealing to Mr Greaves for sympathy now.

—Yes, yes, can't you see the signature? said Mr Greaves. It's definitely Greaves, or Grieves. The waters at the World's End! That's Ayrshire, which I'm pretty positive now is where we first came to light!

Mrs Greaves had her eyes fixed on the mud and slowly lapping water at her feet, for she could no longer bear to look at the lovely old watercolours and prints on the walls. In each one of them, indeed, was a frog—larger in some than in others, aggressive and sometimes gentle. They squatted on painted boats, and their heads came popping up out of the river. Her heart was pounding, but she thought she could hear them plop out of the pictures and onto the wet floor, and then back again—or it might have been the frog upstairs jumping about for fun. A tear, at last, oozed from Mrs Greaves's eye and joined the Thames below.

Of course, Mr Greaves was distressed by his wife's state in the end—and alarmed too to find all their works of art menaced by a plague of frogs. Although Griselda's frog had been an acceptable companion for her when it was the only one in the house—a token frog, so to speak—it became less easy to like now there were swarms of them around. And the Greaves were determined to be liberal about this. They told each other endlessly their own credos of love—Mrs Greaves that Griselda had truly fallen in love, that she had chosen the object of her affections with care, that the frog was her only possible life companion, Mr Greaves that their daughter, landed with the frog by mistake when so many suitable young men might have presented themselves in the end, would come to love the frog and make the best of a bad job out of it. Griselda paid no attention to either of them. She stayed in her room, where trays were brought up for Froggy and herself. In a glory of love she lay in bed, while the ugly animal, becoming a part of her as soon as it was attached to her, brought her happiness from her own deepest sources. Downstairs, Mr Greaves hung the print of the well from which Griselda now drank her fill. The Thames went down, the floors were scrubbed, Mrs Greaves moaned over the damage in the cellar. Everything returned to normal.

Everything, that is, except the frog, which on the third morning turned into an extremely handsome young man. It was Griselda's turn to scream in dismay when she awoke to find a head of golden hair rather than a slimy little frog on the pillow beside her. The young man had a straight nose, Prussian blue eyes, and he was wearing a blue suit with a tie. Mr Greaves, who came running at Griselda's call of horror, found him almost too good to be true. Mrs Greaves, who met the young man at breakfast, privately considered him not artistic enough (but was an artist for a husband such a good thing anyway, as she often pondered with the example of Mr Greaves in mind). No, still following their separate beliefs, both Griselda's parents were pleasantly surprised by the young man. He was certainly conventional. But it was a long time since a young man like that had been seen in their part of the world.

Griselda moped for many weeks over the loss of her frog. Even in the photographs of the wedding at Chelsea Old Church she has her old bad-tempered expression on her face again. Two years later, when she was divorced, the Greaves told each other for the hundredth time that they had done everything they could to help Griselda over her silly phase. They had stacked what Mrs Greaves called the 'frog prints' in the cellar (no one would want to buy them now). Griselda had been encouraged to find maturity by being given a lump sum for the maintenance of her marriage. All to no avail! Griselda, back in her parents' home for what appears to be a permanent stay after her disastrous marriage, still mopes for her first and only love, the frog. Sometimes she goes down to the cellar and sits there for hours, going through the old watercolours and prints, searching for the mandrake root which was long ago thrown away, trying to pretend to herself that the clumsy, ill-executed frogs in the prints are her frog in disguise. They aren't, of course. Mr Greaves has thrown out the 'Complaynt for Scotland' and never refers to his ancestry. And as far as the outside world is concerned, Griselda is doing a course in history of art with an old friend of Mrs Greaves.

LYNNE TILLMAN

Boots and Remorse

T HIS STORY HAS a beginning. I have a friend named Amy who, years ago, had seven cats. Not only did she have seven cats, but at the time she also fed strays. I remember her telling me about one cat who lived behind a wall. She would leave food for it in front of a slit in the wall, a hole, and somehow, in the miraculous way cats have, the cat would squeeze through the hole and eat the cat food. Every night Amy made her rounds with cans of cat food, a can opener, and water too, and she would deposit everything at the appropriate though improbable homes and imperceptible feeding holes.

Our family had a cat. Her name was Griselda, and she was a brilliant calico. I didn't know, for example, that you weren't supposed to train cats to sit up and beg, or crawl, but because I was only five and Griselda was compassionate, she let me teach her. She also used to imitate my mother and wear her lipstick, rubbing her thin cat lips on an uncovered lipstick tube, or, uncatlike, she'd only give birth if my mother was in attendance, assisting. When my mother visited friends, Griselda would wait outside their houses, ready to walk her home. The Griselda tale had a sad end, one that still infuriates everyone in my family; I don't want to write it.

I loved cats, but I didn't have one. Amy wanted me to adopt one of the strays she fed. I was resistant, undecided, and guilty, since every night she'd go out and care for animals I supposedly loved but did not provide a home for. With a lot of excitement Amy announced that she had a cat for me, one she'd been feeding since he was born. She said he was the perfect cat for me and she continued: He is the most handsome cat I have ever seen. And the smartest. I told Amy I'd consider him. I was tempted by her high praise, which I never considered might be hyperbolic. It came from someone who'd seen many cats and had many of her own. The smartest. The most handsome.

One night I returned home to find a message from Amy on my answering machine: I've trapped your cat with turkey. I lured him into the cat carrying case and he's in my hallway, I can't bring him into my loft because of the other cats. Call me as soon as you get home, no matter what time it is.

I called her and went right over. In the hall Amy opened a large cat carrying case—she had several that were big enough to take two or more cats in case of fire. A skinny black and white cat with a pink nose and long face emerged. He was terrified, dirty, and scrawny, and he was ugly. Anyway I thought he was ugly, and I don't like cats with pink noses, but there Amy was, standing next to me, and she thought he was handsome. I couldn't say anything. We were in a sense both trapped in a sort of arranged marriage. I told Amy I liked him. He became my cat. I named him Boots because of his best feature, his white paws.

Amy says that it didn't happen this way. She says, first, she brought me to the car under which Boots lived, to view him, and then, when he came out, terrified, scrawny, and dirty, and in my eyes ugly, I was unenthusiastic. But this, Amy explains now, did not deter her; that is, she knew I didn't want Boots, but she trapped him anyway.

Boots and I reached my loft, or office. I was living on the sixteenth floor of an office building on John Street. We residentials were illegal tenants, sharing the building strangely with jewelers and other businesses forced to tolerate us. As soon as I opened the cat carrying case, Boots jumped out and ran crazily around the room until he found a hiding place. He disappeared for at least a week. I put food out and left the room, and when I returned, it would have been eaten, but I never saw him. It was as if he weren't there. I hated him but he was my cat.

It was the end of summer. I was working at a job that I also hated. As I was addressing envelopes for a bulk mailing, I realized with a tremendous shock that I had left my windows open, wide open, and that Boots, the cat I hated and had never even petted, that Boots might leap out and fall sixteen stories and land splat on the street, and die. And it would be my fault. Melancholic, I began to think about Boots, what a nice cat he was, how scared he was and what a terrible person I was, so unfeeling, ruled by an aesthetic that excluded pink noses and so on. I thought I would die until I returned home. Finally, breathlessly, I did. I looked out the windows and down and I looked all around the room and even behind the refrigerator. There he was. My Boots, alive. How I loved him. He didn't become a lap cat or even an affectionate animal, but he started to come around, and when David, a musician, moved in with me, Boots took to him.

David says that I did not find Boots immediately. He says that I arrived home in a panic, and when I couldn't find Boots anywhere, I telephoned Amy. She advised me to move the refrigerator. And there he was.

Boots liked David, who was and is much more patient than I. David taught him how to play, for instance. Life went on, and Boots began to sleep under the covers next to David, which for a cat shows trust. Boots loved David; I don't think he ever forgave me for my initial lack of interest.

There were many reasons he might have had for not forgiving me. One night I came home drunk. I don't actually remember doing it, but I found another black and white cat on the street, picked him up, carried him home, and he terrorized Boots. By the time David returned—which was and is usually late, musician time—I was asleep, dead to everything. The cats were engaged in territorial combat, and they kept David up all night. It must have been pretty strange for David, two black and white cats where there had been just one, mirror images screaming and racing around the apartment. We gave the cat away the next day and I don't remember exactly how or to whom.

David says that he did not stay up all night. He says he woke me right away and forced me to take the other cat downstairs, to the street, where I'd found it.

Sheila lived on the sixteenth floor too—she had a cat named Ocean—and we were making a film together. After five years, we were finally editing the film. By then Sheila had moved away and David and I had also moved, with Boots, to East Tenth Street. The first night in our new apartment Boots was so terrified that he didn't come out from under the blankets. He also didn't move for the next day or two. He stayed absolutely still while the neighbors downstairs yelled murderously at each other.

Boots adjusted gradually to his new home. The more I think about him, the more I realize how insecure and disturbed he was. Which makes the story I'm telling even more heartbreaking and me even more horrible. But I'll go on.

Sheila and I were editing our movie in an office on John Street, where we'd once lived, and one day, before starting to work, we went to Chinatown for dim sum. Leaving the restaurant, we encountered a black and white cat who came out from under a parked car and followed us. He was so short and stocky, he looked no more than ten months old, a kitten, I thought. Sheila said we had to rescue him. She grabbed the cat, which was easy—he didn't resist, he wanted to go with us—and carried him wrapped in her jacket all the way back to the editing room. Once we were there and settled into our editing positions, Sheila at the controls, me behind her in another chair, the cat settled into his position on my lap. He was more than a lap cat, he was a rug, since he didn't so much sit on my lap as cling to it.

I knew I had to have him and so I went home that night and began telling David about the new cat and how adorable he was and how we had to have him and how Boots would one day adapt to him and how he would like a friend and how we couldn't put him back on the street, how cruel that was, and how I loved him. David was adamant. No, never, one cat, that's all, not another cat, you can't do this to Boots. I already knew Boots didn't want a companion since he didn't like company, and scarcely wanted to be with us—or with me, anyway.

I had to have the new cat. Every night, after working in the editing room where the little stocky fellow was alternately loving and angry, but always clinging and needy, I pleaded with David. I did this for a month until David, enervated and exhausted with saying no, reluctantly agreed. He resigned himself to it, but he was, and remained, against the idea. It was greater than stubbornness. David identified with Boots. It was as if I were bringing a new man, a lover, into our home. This made David and Boots even closer.

David says he never agreed. He says that his music workshop teacher died around this time and he was depressed, in mourning. He says I took advantage of his weakness.

I brought the new cat home and named him Tuba after the latest instrument David was playing. I suppose I was hoping to inveigle the cat Tuba into David's musician heart just through its name, a cheap shot which did not melt David. He viewed Tuba as an interloper and a threat, to Boots and to himself. I was the engineer, the agent, of this destruction; I was breaking up our home and staying in it. If she could do this, I felt David felt, she could do anything. David paid even more attention to Boots to compensate for my sin. He hardly even looked at Tuba and almost never petted him.

The most important thing, though, was how Boots reacted to and treated Tuba, how they got along. They fought, of course, all cats fight with each other initially. And although Boots was furious, attacking, and ferocious, Tuba, from the very beginning, was imperturbable, indifferent, and fearless. Tuba's ears were notched, marked by many battles; he had a hairless scar on his thigh from a car accident or a devastating and calamitous catfight. He was, let's say, streetwise and cocky. Tuba did not seem to have any worries about Boots, the older, much bigger cat whose territory he was invading. This must have further disheartened Boots, who was, as I've already described, insecure, paranoid, and long-suffering.

On Tuba's first night with us, Boots slept, as usual, under the covers next to David. I awoke to discover Tuba sleeping snuggled into the crook of my arm, with his head on my shoulder. From the start, Tuba wasn't afraid to be on the bed even though it was Boots's place. In cat parlance, I believe we humans were to Boots the dominant cats, especially since we provided food for him, but Tuba was neither wary of us nor concerned about Boots. He assumed his place immediately. After a while, Tuba liked to sleep on top of Boots as he lay under the covers. What Boots made of that I don't know. He may have been indignant.

Tuba annoyed Boots. The younger cat wanted to play with him and liked to tease him. No matter how many times Boots let Tuba know he wasn't interested, that he didn't like him or want to play, Tuba insisted. He was unstoppable. Jauntily, insouciantly, Tuba always came back for more. Unlike Boots, Tuba is sure of himself. Overall, Boots was, I think, immune to Tuba's charm.

Four years passed. Boots was becoming stranger and

stranger; I now know this in retrospect. It's that imperceptible thing, like the slits in walls cats can squeeze through,
how you can live with someone, a friend, a lover, a cat, and
not recognize, because they're so close, or that's what one
tells oneself, because one has a stake in not knowing, most
likely, not recognize what's happening to that cat, that lover,
that friend.

More and more, strange noises disturbed Boots. Increasingly, strangers coming into the house angered him. Everything upset him. I didn't put it all, pull it all, together. There
were incidents that seemed isolated, at first. My friend Diane
came over to give me a shiatsu massage; Boots went for her
legs. She was shaken. I played it down. Boots even went for
David's legs once, but not badly. I became wary about having
friends over because I didn't know what Boots would do. (It's
a strange worry: Should I ask so-and-so over; what if Boots
attacks?) Incidents were building one on top of the other, but
then Boots would be fine for days on end. So I'd push away
the bad event, already a memory, and decide it was an anom-
aly after all. Then, suddenly, he'd get weird or crazy again. It
was like having a mad dog in the house except it was a cat.
Chat lunatique. Boots was changing for the worse, and life
with him was extreme and unpleasant in the extreme, at least
for me—he and David had a good relationship still, which
was not easy to bear. I didn't know what was happening to
Boots, what to name it, or what to do about him, and because I didn't I tried not to think about it. Boots had his
good days.

David reminds me that when his friend Wayne, another
musician, visited, Boots jumped up into the cupboard and,

from all the many jars and cans, threw down a can of his cat food. Wayne thought Boots was a genius. David led Wayne to believe he did too.

One Sunday the doorbell rang. It was the upstairs neighbor. She needed something. I walked away to get it but when I walked back, to give it to her, Boots leaped out and dug all his claws into my left calf. He hung onto and clung to my bare leg, with his claws, with an insane ferocity. The neighbor stood and stared as I tore him off me. I watched tissue oozing from the bloody holes dug deep in my leg. All the fur on Boots's body stood out. He seemed double his size. I poured hydrogen peroxide on my calf and found Band-Aids. I had been intending to meet my friend Craig for dinner. I wanted to cancel but Craig wasn't well, had AIDS, and I didn't think I could cancel because of my cat's attacking me. It sounded an unlikely, insignificant, and bizarre excuse.

At the restaurant my calf started to swell and since I tend to imagine the worst, not unlike Boots, I suppose, I was distracted and worried, and also feeling immensely stupid, almost feebleminded. Luckily a doctor Craig knew was in the restaurant and I asked him if I had to get a shot, and he said I didn't, unless it looked very bad the next day. I now can't remember if I went for a shot. I still have small depressions in my calf where Boots's claws dug in, though.

Before Craig died in 1990, he had a cat for about a year. Craig discovered the cat on a rainy, miserable day, lying in a box in a garbage can in front of the brownstone where he lived. Craig wasn't sure if she was dead or not, and he asked me to go downstairs and see if she was still lying there. I carried her from the garbage pail up five flights of stairs to his apartment. She moved, was alive, so I brought her to a vet near Craig, for a checkup and shots. Craig named her Miss Kitty after the woman in "Gunsmoke."

In the beginning Craig was anxious about whether Miss Kitty was happy or not. I think she was. She rewarded Craig with affection and devotion, spending most of her time lying next to him on his bed. Craig was less lonely because of her. Toward the end he couldn't care for her anymore, and I helped find her a home. That was a sad story too. Craig never knew it didn't work out exactly as planned, but Miss Kitty at least did find a home, even if it wasn't the intended one.

Now that Boots had attacked me, badly, something had to be done. It was obvious. Boots was watching my every move. The farther from the bed I walked, the more alarmed Boots became. He would follow me, stalk me, his fur sticking out from his body. He'd walk very close to my legs. I was afraid, and to be afraid of a domestic animal is disorienting. First of all, you feel insane being terrified of your pet and everyone else finds it funny. Even I thought it was funny in a way. Tuba noticed nothing, I think.

I telephoned the vet I trusted—she had discovered what four others had not: Tuba had an obstruction that was causing his constipation, which meant he had to eat baby food mixed with fiber softener for the rest of his life. I described Boots's behavior. She said that some people had had success with a pet therapist, whose number she gave me. I assumed a pet therapist was an animal trainer, a behavior-modification trainer. I made an appointment.

Boots behaved himself for days before the appointment

and I began to think it was unnecessary. But the doorbell rang at ten A.M. as planned. I went downstairs to let the pet therapist in. She was wearing a yellow slicker and hat, had come on a bike, and was very short, like an elf.

She and I walked the four flights to my door and when I opened it, Boots assumed an attack position not ten feet from us. He wasn't going to let her in. It was uncanny. He'd never done this before; I'm sure he knew why she was there. For about ten minutes she stood in the doorway, making cutchy-cutchy-coo noises to Bootsy-wootsy. Boots, his fur all fluffed out, was unmoved. She said again and again, He wants to attack. Yes, I said.

David was in the shower; he was leaving for a tour in Germany later that day. Our apartment is a large railroad, and the only room with a door is the bathroom. When the shower water stopped running, the pet therapist said: Get David to distract Boots, to call him, and then have David put him in the bathroom and shut the door. David distracted Boots, put him in the bathroom, shut the door, and she was able to enter our apartment. We sat down at the kitchen table while Boots meowed in the bathroom. David packed.

First the pet therapist instructed me to record on audio-tape what was spoken in the session. In addition she asked me to play a tape of Keith Jarrett–like music which she had brought, so that the music would also be recorded as back-ground to her voice. All of this I did.

Then she opened her writing pad and inquired about Boots's history. I was in analysis at the time and not unfamil-iar with the kinds of questions she was asking, although, with the putative patient locked in the bathroom, this was irregular. I was impatient but trying hard to take her and the process seriously since this might be Boots's only chance.

I narrated the sad story of Boots's life, where he was born, how Amy fed and then trapped him, that he was paranoid, that I was the one who brought Tuba in, that Boots loved David more than me, and on and on. I kept expecting that soon she would open the bathroom door and do something with Boots, begin to retrain him or talk to him at least. The more I related to her—Boots didn't trust me, I had betrayed him—the more I felt I had destroyed Boots, just as David told me I would. I spoke for about twenty minutes, answering all her questions to the best of my ability. Then she said that she was going to write up her assessment and, while she did, I could read an article about her. It was in *The New Yorker,* a Talk of the Town column. Apparently she'd had some success with a large, unhappy grey cat and appeared to have been taken seriously by several of her clients. By the time I finished reading the favorable, only mildly ironic story, the pet therapist had finished her analysis of Boots.

She looked penetratingly, steadily, into my eyes. Gravely she explained that Boots was suffering from "kitten deprivation syndrome." Then she gave me instructions. I was to play the tape of her voice for Boots three times a day, to calm him. Since Boots loved David, she asked if David would say something to Boots on the tape, a message Boots could listen to so that he would know David was coming back. David was still packing, dressed in his terry cloth robe; I brought him to his studio area, where she asked him to record his personal message to Boots. I believe he said, with an aggrieved smile: Hey, Boots, I'll see you later, man.

She wanted me to call her in a few days. Then she left.

But before she left I paid her. Eighty dollars. Everyone always wants to know that. To me that was insignificant, the least of it. I telephoned the vet and complained. I never thought that when the vet said "pet therapist" she meant that. The vet suggested Valium and having Boots's front claws removed. I agreed. The alternative was worse.

Some time after that, Boots went for my legs again and even without his front claws, he ripped the skin. And he received a greeting card from the pet therapist, addressed to "Sir Boots Tillman." The card had a picture of a happy cat on the cover. On the inside, in a scrawl, she wrote her message: "Dear Sir Boots, Don't worry, everything's going to be all right. Signed, Sunny Blue the Wizard."

David left again for a tour in Canada, just a weekend, but I would have to be alone with Boots. Boots and Tuba. Tuba was hardly a comfort when he was one of the reasons Boots hated me.

By the way, during this period of extreme desperation, and out of curiosity as much as anything else, I did once play the pet therapist's tape for Boots, who, of course, ignored it. I also gave him Valium and took some myself.

While David was out of town, late on the Saturday night of a Fourth of July weekend filled with loud bangs and blasts, Boots jumped up onto the kitchen table. All his hair fluffed out and his head rolled from side to side on his neck. His eyes, as big and round as headlights, followed me like radar. It was something like the effect in *The Exorcist* when Linda Blair's head spun around. Boots was bigger than ever. Somehow I found the courage to grab him by the neck, throw him into the bathroom, and close the door. Boots hated the bathroom because that was his room for punishment, for isolation. But I was afraid to sleep with him near me. I thought he might go for my eyes. I'd seen that in a movie.

I awoke in the middle of the night to find Boots sleeping not on the bed beside me but on the floor next to the bed. That was startling. First of all, how had he gotten out of the bathroom?

The night before I had taken the precaution of bringing his cat carrier down, just in case. I decided to get out of bed, to move very slowly, not to alarm Boots, and walk to it. I wanted to shove Boots into it and keep him there, locked inside, until David came home. As I walked toward the carrier, Boots began stalking me, his fur thickening and fluffing. I grabbed him by the scruff of his neck and stuffed him into the case. I did this very quickly, in one motion, as if I had trained for it. Then, terrified, I telephoned David in Canada and demanded that as soon as he returned he take Boots to the animal hospital, to have him killed. I could write, to have him put to sleep, but killed is right. I would keep Boots in his case until then.

The next night, Sunday, David arrived home. It was late. He put his suitcase and bass down and with barely any words between us, he lifted the cat case and left. He was gone about two hours and when he returned, without Boots, I cried. I sobbed, I think. David had held Boots while the doctor injected him. David said Boots's eyes rolled back into his head. He died instantly.

David says it didn't happen this way. He says that he came home early on Sunday morning, but I was out of town, on Long Island for the Fourth of July. He took Boots out of the case and they spent a relaxed and happy day together.

When I arrived home, late, and saw Boots out of his carrying case, I insisted that David take him, right then and there, to be killed. Murderer, David says now, half-seriously.

Craig died early on the morning of a Fourth of July two years later. My mother wanted me to incorporate all her Griselda stories into my Boots story. I told her I might.

In case I ever forget, there are photographs of Boots and Tuba sitting next to each other. The sun is shining brightly on them, their bodies casting long shadows on the floor. Both cats are looking at the camera, serenely, as if posing for a formal portrait. They seem peaceful, even content. They were known to groom each other on occasion and even to nap next to each other, but they always fought. Boots may have been going senile. He may have had a brain tumor. There are explanations, one can look for and find explanations, but I don't know. I can't explain what happened.

GUY TREBAY

Three Bears

TWO VISITORS AT the Central Park Zoo:
  "See, the big one must be the man and the little one is the female. She's lying there and he's doting on her. Do you see that, Sam?"
  "Why is he doing that?"
  "He hopes she'll have a baby."
  "Where's the other one?"
  "The other what?"
  "The man said there were three bears."
  "It's over there on a rock."
  "Is that a female?"
  "I don't know."
  "That's a sad polar bear, Mommy. She's sniffling like I am."

Gus, the male, has a squarish head with ears set well back on the skull, a long muzzle, and a massive trunk. He's densely furred, especially on his shaggy underbelly. The flesh on Gus's hind parts seems to fit him loosely; from the rear he resembles a baggy pants comedian. Lily, the young female, has a compact muzzle and large moth-eaten ears. Today, in the weak sun of a warm, dim February afternoon, she is circling a large group of imitation boulders with Gus in pursuit. First she paces up and down on a stone ledge. Then she moves around the scored rim of the big gray rocks. Then she flattens herself to the stone, dipping muzzle to water, and sips. She does this delicately, without wariness and then, as if she's just realized someone was watching, lifts herself up and glides out of sight. Her entire performance has a kind of contained dignity, especially considering that, twenty feet away, behind glass windows, a handful of visitors is spying on her every move. Gus is also watching, from around the corner. Ida is also watching, from an outcrop thirty feet away.

A keeper:

"They're named Ida, Lily, and Gus. The females are five and six. The male is five. One female's from Buffalo. The other's from Germany. Some people around here call her Germany or Lily Marlene. The male's from Toledo. The breeding season is pretty short. How can you tell they're in season? Well, the female is somewhat receptive, a little more playful. There's not that much courtship to speak of. If it worked, there should be a cub in November.

Three visitors:

"This one looks like he wants a beer and a couple of pretzels."

"That water looks cold."

"He says, 'Give me a cigarette and the remote.'"

"Look, he's taking a drink. Look how he's balancing on the edge of that rock. He might fall in, you know."

"That one seems dirty. He's got a dirty butt."

"He says, 'Is Monday Night Football on?'"

"How does their fur get so yellow?"

"Probably pollution. Whoa, did you see those claws?"

"Now they're kissing or something. He's licking her. What is that? Her belly?"

"Hey, look at that. That's rude."

"Don't you think they should give them a private place to do that?"

"Like what? Book a room at a motel?"

"Do you think they might fall in that freezing water?"

"Yeah! Jump, polar bears. Jump!"

"Don't shout or you're going to scare them."

"Hey, we better go look at the seals."

Conversation with a keeper:

"Are polar bears endangered?"

"They're a threatened species."

"How do they decide which is which?"

"There's a whole set of requirements before a breed passes from one state to the next."

"Has this pair bred yet?"

"We think so."

"And so it's over for this year."

"Passed yesterday. There's just some residual behavior now."

"It seems like everyone at the zoo can feel spring coming on."

"Well, the whooper swans will be starting courtship in a couple of weeks, I guess."

"And what about the monkeys? They were really going at it up on a rock."

"Oh, the monkeys. They're pretty much always like that."

A high school group:

"Let's look at the bears next."

"Wait, I want to see if the macaques are gonna screw."

"Sean!"

"Look, he's going up on her from behind."

"Gross! That monkey just pooped."

"How come their butts are red like that?"

"It's for sexual attraction, like lipstick."

"I don't exactly put lipstick on my rear."

"That's not what I heard."

"Ha-ha, Sean. Very funny."

"Did you see the Naturemax movie at the Museum of Natural History? They showed these same monkeys taking hot baths in Japan."

"Really?"

"Yeah. In, like, mineral springs from a volcano."

"Look, now that one monkey is chasing her around. The one that was on a branch."

"Yo, monkey, party on!"

"Do you think she wants it and she's playing hard to get?"

"Sean, don't be such a sexist."

"Look, he got her. Schwing!"

A child and her mother:

"It says here that polar bears travel along the Arctic ice pack for nine months a year."

"What do they eat on the ice?"

"Fish, I would think. Oh, it says here they eat mostly seals. The polar bears catch the seals and eat just the skin and the blubber. Then they leave the rest on the ice and it provides food for other animals."

"What animals?"

"Arctic fox."

"What do these bears eat?"

"Fish."

"Mommy! The bears are kissing."

Two friends:

"Do you think bears have a god?"

"No."

"Why not?"

"If they did, he wouldn't stick them here in this fake North Pole."

"I think this tank is beautiful, with the glass and the rocks and whatever."

"I guess."

"Anyway, why should a bear god be any kinder than the human one?"

"I don't know. Because animals aren't stained with original sin?"

"Oh, look, the female's presenting."

"Let's go."

"I want to watch."

"Let' s go."

"What's your problem?"

"I just think we might give them the dignity of screwing in peace."

Two bears:

Gus and Lily touch snouts. Ida is still on her rock. Lily slumps her bulk against a boulder and retracts one leg, giving Gus access to her abdomen, which he sniffs. The male smells and then inspects the female for several moments. He seems to drink her perfume. Then the female shuts her legs and spreads herself prone. Gus mounts her, but not sexually. He presses the length of his body against Lily's, spoonwise, and they doze.

A young girl (hands cupped to the glass):

"Bears, can you hear me? Yoo-hoo, bears. Hello, bears. Wake up."

WILLIAM WEGMAN

Man Ray

S INCE 1970 I have been known as "the guy with the
dog." I didn't want a dog. I got Man Ray for my wife
Gayle. She wanted one. I was too busy being an artist
to have a dog.

In 1970, we had just moved to L.A. and I was making
conceptual art with a camera. I was photographing constructed scenes from everyday life, ordinary things around
the house: doing dishes, the light switch on and off, hot and
cold water, Gayle dropping a glass of milk, me tasting wine.
Some of the photographs had accompanying texts. I got a
job teaching drawing at Cal State Long Beach, and borrowed
objects from the still-life locker for my photos. One of my
students, Tim Owen, was married to a twin, Lynn. I photographed her and her sister, Terry. I had also just purchased
my own video equipment: a CV Sony with a GE nameplate
on it, a recorder with a surveillance-type camera, and a black
and white reel-to-reel–type VTR. In Madison, Wisconsin,
where I had been teaching, I had borrowed video equipment.

But a promise is a promise, and I had promised Gayle
that we would get a dog when we moved from Wisconsin to
L.A. She wanted a dalmation. So one day I brought home a

six-week-old Weimaraner. We didn't know what to do with it so we put it on the bed and took its picture. Not unlike a baby's first family picture. I remember watching him sleep next to a speaker blaring the music of Stockhausen and setting up my video camera to tape him. He looked great on video. I put the camera on the floor and poured milk out of my mouth as I backed away from it into the next room. As I disappeared, Ray appeared to lick up the milk, steadily consuming the puddle until he bumped into the camera. I moved him to another place on the floor where I had poured another puddle of milk, and photographed him while he drank. I moved him again, to a place on the floor where the floorboards ran perpendicular to the floorboards in the previous picture. These two photographs became a diptych. I videotaped him chewing on a microphone and recorded the sound.

Did I get him too early? Taking him away from his mother at six weeks—rather than the recommended eight to twelve—did Man Ray become overly dependent on me? I really liked working with him but he seemed to need my constant attention. For me to photograph or videotape him was a form of heightened attention, literally focusing on him. He emitted a high frequency whine that drove me crazy when I was working with other props and subjects. Usually I would give in to him. Some of my students at Cal State Long Beach suggested I get rid of him. "He's ruining your life." It's true he started taking over my life little by little and sometimes I resented that. More often I liked it. To alleviate some of the dependency problem, Gayle and I decided to get him a dog. A German short-haired pointer we named Art. Big mistake. Art lasted two weeks with us before we gave him to a friend who moved to a farm in Ohio and saved his life. Man Ray was a whining prima donna until he was a year and a half old and then suddenly he was cool. He was a joy to be around; as entertaining in life as he appeared in photography and video.

At a certain point I began to question my use of him. Was he becoming a crutch? I vowed to use him sparingly. The last thing I wanted was a trademark and I dreaded sentimentality. Only the best for Man Ray. I edited the video especially, severely weeding out cuteness and fluff. Being cute was not Ray's style. His being gray made it easy for me to return to him repeatedly with new ideas. He was like a blackboard in that way. How many things can you do with a dalmation?

During the second year of working together he took notice of the camera and lighting equipment, realizing that when this stuff was around we were going to be doing something specific. It involved play but was not play. It was work. In that second year we had moved to the Venice–Santa Monica area, out of a little duplex in San Pedro with charming household features and into a "real" artist's studio with white walls and high ceilings. In the new space I set him in different positions on wooden boxes in minimal permutations. I had to learn more about photography. I kept screwing up. We had to do it over and over until I got it right. The act of repetition turned us into professionals. In video the process became quite interesting. I would talk to Man Ray in the language he knew. "Do you want to go to the beach . . . for a bike ride . . . do you want to go to the park . . . see Gayle? Teddy?" But there would be a delay. We wouldn't be going right away. First we had to see the recording. At times I had to change words as he would quickly become immune to them. Once in a while he would look directly into the lens of the camera. This occurs noticeably in *Spelling Lesson,* reel four, 1973. Sometimes during a scary movie I turn around to look at the beam of projected light for reassurance.

Man Ray and I worked together for over eleven years. One year (1978) I abstained. We were both miserable. In 1979, I started taking twenty-by-twenty-four Polaroid pictures with him at the Polaroid studio in Boston. The situation there was focused on him. He liked being the center of attention. I noticed that he was getting old and in an incredibly short time I took his last picture. He died March 27, 1982.

JOY WILLIAMS

The Killing Game

D EATH AND SUFFERING are a big part of hunting. A big part. Not that you'd ever know it by hearing hunters talk. They tend to downplay the killing
part. To kill is to put to death, extinguish, nullify, cancel, destroy. But from the hunter's point of view, it's just a tiny part
of the experience. *The kill is the least important part of the
hunt . . .* they often say, or, *Killing involves only a split second of the innumerable hours we spend surrounded by and observing nature. . . .* For the animal, of course, the killing
part is of considerably more importance. Jose Ortega y
Gasset, in *Meditations on Hunting,* wrote, *Death is a sign of
reality in hunting. One does not hunt in order to kill; on the
contrary, one kills in order to have hunted.* This is the sort of
intellectual blather that the "thinking" hunter holds dear.
The conservation editor of *Field & Stream,* George Reiger,
recently paraphrased this sentiment by saying, *We kill to
hunt, and not the other way around,* thereby making it truly
fatuous. A hunter in West Virginia, one Mr. Bill Neal, blazed
through this philosophical fog by explaining why he blows
the toes off tree raccoons so that they will fall down and be
torn apart by his dogs. *That's the best part of it. It's not any
fun just shooting them.*

Instead of monitoring animals—many animals in managed areas are tagged, tattooed, and wear radio transmitters—wildlife managers should start hanging telemetry gear around hunters' necks to study their attitudes and listen to their conversations. It would be grisly listening, but it would tune out for good the *suffering as sacrament* and *spiritual experience* blather that some hunting apologists employ. *The unease with which the good hunter inflicts death is an unease not merely with his conscience but with affirming his animality in the midst of his struggles toward humanity and clarity,* Holmes Rolston III drones on in his book *Environmental Ethics.*

There is a formula to this in literature—someone the protagonist loves has just died, so he goes out and kills an animal. This makes him feel better. But it's kind of a sad feeling-better. He gets to relate to Death and Nature in this way. Somewhat. But not really. Death is still a mystery. Well, it's hard to explain. It's sort of a semireligious thing. . . . Killing and affirming, affirming and killing, it's just the cross the "good" hunter must bear. The bad hunter just has to deal with postkill letdown.

Many are the hunter's specious arguments. Less semireligious but a long-standing favorite with them is the vegetarian approach (you eat meat, don't you?). If you say no, they feel they've got you—you're just a vegetarian attempting to impose your weird views on others. If you say yes, they accuse you of being hypocritical, of allowing your genial A&P butcher to stand between you and reality. The fact is, the chief attraction of hunting is the pursuit and murder of animals—the meat-eating aspect of it is trivial. If the hunter chooses to be *ethical* about it he might cook his kill, but the meat of most animals is discarded. Dead bear can even be dangerous! A bear's heavy hide must be skinned at once to prevent meat spoilage. With effort, a hunter can make okay chili, *something to keep in mind,* a sports rag says, *if you take two skinny spring bears.*

As for subsistence hunting, please. . . . Granted that there might be one "good" hunter out there who conducts the kill as spiritual exercise and two others who are atavistic enough to want to supplement their Chicken McNuggets with venison, most hunters hunt for the hell of it.

For hunters, hunting is fun. Recreation is play. Hunting is recreation. Hunters kill for play, for entertainment. They kill for the thrill of it, to make an animal "theirs." (The Gandhian doctrine of nonpossession has never been a big hit with hunters.) The animal becomes the property of the hunter by its death. Alive, the beast belongs only to itself. This is unacceptable to the hunter. *He's yours. . . . He's mine. . . . I decided to. . . . I decided not to. . . . I debated shooting it, then I decided to let it live. . . .* Hunters like beautiful creatures. A "beautiful" deer, elk, bear, cougar, bighorn sheep. A "beautiful" goose or mallard. Of course, they don't stay "beautiful" for long, particularly the birds. Many birds become rags in the air, shredded, blown to bits. *Keep shooting till they drop!* Hunters get a thrill out of seeing a plummeting bird, out of seeing it crumple and fall. *The big pheasant folded in classic fashion.* They get a kick out of "collecting" new species. *Why not add a unique harlequin duck to your collection?* Swan hunting is satisfying. *I let loose a three-inch magnum. The large bird only flinched with my first shot and began to gain altitude. I frantically ejected the round, chambered another, and dropped the swan with my second shot. After retrieving the bird I was amazed by its size. The swan's six-foot wingspan, huge body, and long neck made it an impressive trophy.* Hunters like big animals, trophy animals. A "trophy" usually means that the hunter doesn't deign to eat it. Maybe he skins it or mounts it. Maybe he takes a picture. *We took pictures, we took pictures.* Maybe he just looks at it for a while. The disposition of the "experience" is up to the hunter. He's entitled to do whatever he wishes with the damn thing. It's dead.

Hunters like categories they can tailor to their needs. There are the "good" animals—deer, elk, bear, moose—which are allowed to exist for the hunter's pleasure. Then there are the "bad" animals, the vermin, varmints, and "nuisance" animals, the rabbits and raccoons and coyotes and beavers and badgers, which are disencouraged to exist. The hunter can have fun killing them, but the pleasure is diminished because the animals aren't "magnificent."

Then there are the predators. These can be killed any time, because, hunters argue, they're predators, for godssakes.

Many people in South Dakota want to exterminate the red fox because it preys upon some of the ducks and pheasant they want to hunt and kill each year. They found that after they killed the wolves and coyotes, they had more foxes than they wanted. The ring-necked pheasant is South Dakota's state bird. No matter that it was imported from Asia specifically to be "harvested" for sport, it's South Dakota's state bird and they're proud of it. A group called Pheasants Unlimited gave some tips on how to hunt foxes. *Place a small amount of larvicide* [a grain fumigant] *on a rag and chuck it down the hole. . . . The first pup generally comes out in fif-*

teen minutes. . . . Use a .22 to dispatch him. . . . Remove each pup shot from the hole. Following gassing, set traps for the old fox who will return later in the evening. . . . Poisoning, shooting, trapping—they make up a sort of sportsman's triathalon.

In the hunting magazines, hunters freely admit the pleasure of killing to one another. *Undeniable pleasure radiated from her smile. The excitement of shooting the bear had Barb talking a mile a minute.* But in public, most hunters are becoming a little wary about raving on as to how much fun it is to kill things. Hunters have a tendency to call large animals by cute names—"bruins" and "muleys," "berry-fed blackies" and "handsome cusses" and "big guys," thereby implying a balanced jolly game of mutual satisfaction between hunter and the hunted—*Bam, bam, bam, I get to shoot you and you get to be dead.* More often, though, when dealing with the nonhunting public, a drier, businesslike tone is employed. Animals become a "resource" that must be "utilized." Hunting becomes "a legitimate use of the resource." Animals become a product like wool or lumber or a crop like fruit or corn that must be "collected" or "taken" or "harvested." Hunters love to use the word *legitimate.* (Oddly, Tolstoy referred to hunting as "evil legitimized.") *A legitimate use, a legitimate form of recreation, a legitimate escape, a legitimate pursuit.* It's a word they trust will slam the door on discourse. Hunters are increasingly relying upon their spokesmen and supporters, state and federal game managers and wildlife officials, to employ the drone of a solemn bureaucratic language and toss around a lot of questionable statistics to assure the non-hunting public (93 percent!) that there's nothing to worry about. The pogrom is under control. The mass murder and manipulation of wild animals is just another business. Hunters are a tiny minority, and it's crucial to them that the millions of people who don't hunt not be awakened from their long sleep and become antihunting. Nonhunters are okay. Dweeby, probably, but okay. A hunter *can respect the rights* of a nonhunter. It's the "antis" he despises, those *misguided, emotional, not-in-possession-of-the-facts, uninformed zealots who don't understand nature. . . . Those dimestore ecologists cloaked in ignorance and spurred by emotion. . . . Those doggy-woggy types, who under the guise of being environmentalists and conservationists are working to deprive him of his precious right to kill.* (Sometimes it's just a *right*; sometimes it's a *God-given* right.) Antis can be scorned, but nonhunters must be pacified, and this is where the number crunching of wildlife biologists and the scripts of *professional resource managers* come in. Leave it to the professionals. They know what numbers are the good numbers. Utah determined that there were six hundred sandhill cranes in the state, so permits were issued to shoot one hundred of them. Don't want to have too many sandhill cranes. California wildlife officials reported "sufficient numbers" of mountain lions to "justify" renewed hunting, even though it doesn't take a rocket scientist to know the animal is extremely rare. (It's always a dark day for hunters when an animal is adjudged *rare*. How can its numbers be "controlled" through hunting if it scarcely exists? . . .) A recent citizens' referendum prohibits the hunting of the mountain lion in perpetuity—not that the lions aren't killed anyway, in California and all over the West, hundreds of them annually by the government as part of the scandalous Animal Damage Control Program. Oh, to be the lucky hunter who gets to be an official government hunter and can legitimately kill animals his buddies aren't supposed to! Montana officials, led by K. L. Cool, that state's wildlife director, have definite ideas on the number of buffalo they feel can be tolerated. Zero is the number. Yellowstone National Park is the only place in America where bison exist, having been annihilated everywhere else. In the winter of 1988, nearly six hundred buffalo wandered out of the north boundary of the park and into Montana, where they were immediately shot at pointblank range by lottery-winning hunters. It was easy. And it was obvious from a video taken on one of the blow-away-the-bison days that the hunters had a heck of a good time. The buffalo, Cool says, threaten ranchers' livelihood by doing damage to property—by which he means, I guess, that they eat the grass. Montana wants zero buffalo; it also wants zero wolves.

Large predators—including grizzlies, cougars, and wolves—are often the most "beautiful," the smartest and wildest animals of all. The gray wolf is both a supreme predator and an endangered species, and since the Supreme Court recently affirmed that ranchers have no constitutional right to kill endangered predators—apparently some God-given rights are not constitutional ones—this makes the wolf a more or less lucky dog. But not for long. A small population of gray wolves has recently established itself in north-western Montana, primarily in Glacier National Park, and there is a plan, long a dream of conservationists, to "reintroduce" the wolf to Yellowstone. But to please ranchers and hunters, part of the plan would involve immediately removing the wolf from the endangered-species list. Beyond the park's boundaries, he could be hunted as a "game animal" or exterminated as a "pest." (Hunters kill to hunt, remember, except when they're hunting to kill.) The area of Yellowstone where the wolf would be restored is the same mountain and high-plateau country that is abandoned in winter by most animals, including the aforementioned luckless bison. Part of the plan, too, is compensation to ranchers if any of their far-ranging livestock is killed by a wolf. It's a real industry out there, apparently, killing and controlling and getting compensated for losing something under the Big Sky.

Wolves gotta eat—a fact that disturbs hunters. Jack Atcheson, an outfitter in Butte, said, *Some wolves are fine if there is control. But there never will be control. The wolf-control plan provided by the Fish and Wildlife Service speaks only of protecting domestic livestock. There is no plan to protect wildlife. . . . There are no surplus deer or elk in Montana. . . . Their numbers are carefully managed. With uncontrolled wolf populations, a lot of people will have to give up hunting just to feed wolves. Will you give up your elk permit for a wolf?*

It won't be long before hunters start demanding compensation for animals they aren't able to shoot.

Hunters believe that wild animals exist only to satisfy their wish to kill them. And it's so easy to kill them! The weaponry available is staggering, and the equipment and gear limitless. *The demand for big boomers has never been greater than right now,* Outdoor Life *crows, and the makers of rifles and cartridges are responding to the craze with a variety of light artillery that is virtually unprecedented in the history of sporting arms. . . .* Hunters use grossly overpowered shotguns and rifles and compound bows. They rely on four-wheel-drive vehicles and three-wheel ATVs and airplanes. . . . *He was interesting, the only moving, living creature on that limitless white expanse. I slipped a cartridge into the barrel of my rifle and threw the safety off. . . .* They use snowmobiles to run down elk, and dogs to run down and tree cougars. It's easy to shoot an animal out of a tree. It's virtually impossible to miss a moose, a conspicuous and placid animal of steady habits. . . . *I took a deep breath and pulled the trigger. The bull dropped. I looked at my watch: 8:22. The big guy was early. Mike started whooping and hollering and I joined him. I never realized how big a moose was until this one was on the ground. We took pictures. . . .* Hunters shoot animals when they're resting. . . . *Mike selected a deer, settled down to a steady rest, and fired. The buck was his when he squeezed the trigger. John decided to take the other buck, which had jumped up to its feet. The deer hadn't seen us and was confused by the shot echoing about in the valley. John took careful aim, fired, and took the buck. The hunt was over. . . .* And they shoot them when they're eating. . . . *The bruin ambled up the stream, checking gravel bars and backwaters for fish. Finally he plopped down on the bank to eat. Quickly, I tiptoed into range. . . .* They use decoys and calls. . . . *The six point gave me a cold-eyed glare from ninety steps away. I hit him with a 130-grain Sierra boattail handload. The bull went down hard. Our hunt was over. . . .* They use sex lures. . . . *The big buck raised its nose to the air, curled back its lips, and tested the scent of the doe's urine. I held my breath, fought back the shivers, and jerked off a shot. The 180-grain spire-point bullet caught the buck high on the back behind the shoulder and put it down. It didn't get up. . . .* They use walkie-talkies, binoculars, scopes. . . . *With my 308 Browning BLR, I steadied the 9X cross hairs on the front of the bear's massive shoulders and squeezed. The bear cartwheeled backward for fifty yards. . . . The second Federal Premium 165-grain bullet found its mark. Another shot anchored the bear for good. . . .* They bait deer with corn. They spread popcorn on golf courses for Canada geese and they douse meat baits with fry grease and honey for bears. . . . *Make the baiting site redolent of inner-city doughnut shops.* They use blinds and tree stands and mobile stands. They go out in groups, in gangs, and employ "pushes" and "drives." So many methods are effective. So few rules apply. It's fun! . . . *We kept on repelling the swarms of birds as they came in looking for shelter from that big ocean wind, emptying our shell belts. . . .* A species can, in the vernacular, be *pressured by hunting* (which means that killing them has decimated them), but that just increases the fun, the *challenge*. There is practically no criticism of conduct within the ranks. . . . *It's mostly a matter of opinion and how hunters have been brought up to hunt. . . .* Although a recent editorial in *Ducks Unlimited* magazine did venture to primly suggest that one should *not fall victim to greed-induced stress through piggish competition with others.*

But hunters are piggy. They just can't seem to help it. They're overequipped . . . insatiable, malevolent, and vain. They maim and mutilate and despoil. And for the most part, they're inept. Grossly inept.

Camouflaged toilet paper is a must for the modern hunter, along with his Bronco and his beer. Too many hunters taking a dump in the woods with their roll of Charmin beside them were mistaken for white-tailed deer and shot. Hunters get excited. They'll shoot anything—the pallid ass of another sportsman or even themselves. A Long Island man died last year when his shotgun went off as he clubbed a wounded deer with the butt. Hunters get mad. They get restless and want to fire! They want to use those assault rifles and see foamy blood on the ferns. Wounded animals can travel for miles in fear and pain before they collapse. Countless gut-shot deer—*if you hear a sudden, squashy thump, the animal has probably been hit in the abdomen*—are "lost" each year. "Poorly placed shots" are frequent, and injured animals are seldom tracked, because most hunters never learned how to track. The majority of hunters will shoot at anything with four legs during deer season and anything with wings during duck season. Hunters try to nail running animals and distant birds. They become so overeager, so *aroused*, that they misidentify and misjudge, spraying their "game" with shots but failing to bring it down.

The fact is, hunters' lack of skill is a big, big problem. And nowhere is the problem worse than in the new glamour recreation—bow hunting. These guys are elitists. They doll themselves up in camouflage, paint their faces black, and climb up into tree stands from which they attempt the penetration of deer, elk, and turkeys with modern, multiblade, broadhead arrows shot from sophisticated, easy-to-draw compound bows. This "primitive" way of hunting appeals to many, and even the non-hunter may feel that it's a "fairer" method, requiring more strength and skill, but bow hunting is the cruelest, most wanton form of wildlife disposal of all. Studies conducted by state fish and wildlife departments repeatedly show that bow hunters wound and fail to retrieve as many animals as they kill. An animal that flees, wounded by an arrow, will most assuredly die of the wound, but it will be days before he does. Even with a "good" hit, the time elapsed between the strike and death is exceedingly long. *The rule of thumb has long been that we should wait thirty to forty-five minutes on heart and lung hits, an hour or more on a suspected liver hit, eight to twelve hours on paunch hits, and that we should follow immediately on hindquarter and other muscle-only hits, to keep the wound open and bleeding,* is the advice in the magazine *Fins and Feathers*. What the hunter does as he hangs around waiting for his animal to finish with its terrified running and dying hasn't been studied—maybe he puts on more makeup, maybe he has a highball.

Wildlife agencies promote and encourage bow hunting by permitting earlier and longer seasons, even though they are well aware that, in their words, *crippling is a byproduct of the sport,* making archers pretty sloppy for elitists. The broadhead arrow is a very inefficient killing tool. Bow hunters are trying to deal with this problem with the suggestion that they use poison pods. These poisoned arrows are illegal in all states except Mississippi (*Ah'm gonna get ma deer even if ah just nick the little bastard*), but they're widely used anyway. You wouldn't want that deer to suffer, would you?

The mystique of the efficacy and decency of the bow hunter is as much an illusion as the perception that a waterfowler is a refined and thoughtful fellow, a *romantic aesthete,* as Vance Bourjaily put it, equipped with his faithful labs and a love for solitude and wild places. More sentimental drivel has been written about bird shooting than any other type of hunting. It's a soul-wrenching pursuit, apparently, the execution of birds in flight. Ducks Unlimited—an organization that has managed to put a spin on the word *conservation* for years—works hard to project the idea that duck hunters are blue bloods and that duck stamps with their pretty pictures are responsible for saving all the saved puddles in North America. *Sportsman's conservation* is a contradiction in terms (We protect things now so that we can kill them later) and is broadly interpreted (Don't kill them all, just kill most of them). A hunter is conservationist in the same way a farmer or a rancher is: He's not. Like the rancher who kills everything that's not stock on his (and the public's) land, and the farmer who scorns wildlife because "they don't pay their freight," the hunter uses nature by destroying its parts, mastering it by simplifying it through death.

George ("We kill to hunt and not the other way around") Reiger, the conservationist-hunter's spokesman (he's the best they've got, apparently), said that the "dedicated" water-fowler will shoot other game "of course," but *we do so much in the same spirit of the lyrics, that when we're not near the girl we love, we love the girl we're near.* (Duck hunters practice tough love.) The fact is, far from being a "romantic aesthete," the waterfowler is the most avaricious of all hunters . . . *That's when Scott suggested the friendly wager on who would take the most birds* . . . and the most resistant to minimum ecological decency. Millions of birds that managed to elude shotgun blasts were dying each year from ingesting the lead shot that rained down in the wetlands. Year after year, birds perished from feeding on spent lead, but hunters were "re-luctant" to switch to steel. They worried that it would impair their shooting, and ammunition manufacturers said a changeover would be "expensive." State and federal officials had to weigh the poisoning against these considerations. It took forever, this weighing, but now steel-shot loads are re-quired almost everywhere, having been judged "more than adequate" to bring down the birds. This is not to say, of course, that most duck hunters use steel shot almost everywhere. They're traditionalists and don't care for all the new, pesky rules. Oh, for the golden age of waterfowling, when a man could measure a good day's shooting by the pickup load. But those days are gone. Fall is a melancholy time, all right.

Spectacular abuses occur wherever geese congregate, Shooting Sportsman notes quietly, something that the more cultivated Ducks Unlimited would hesitate to admit. Waterfowl populations are plummeting and waterfowl hunters are out of control. "Supervised" hunts are hardly distinguished from unsupervised ones. A biologist with the Department of the Interior who observed a hunt at Sand Lake in South Dakota said, *Hunters repeatedly shot over the line at incoming flights where there was no possible chance of retrieving. Time and time again I was shocked at the behavior of hunters. I heard them laugh at the plight of dazed cripples that stumbled about. I saw them striking the heads of retrieved cripples against fence posts.* In the South, wood ducks return to their roosts after sunset when shooting hours are closed. Hunters find this an excellent time to shoot them. Dennis Anderson, an outdoors writer, said, *Roost shooters just fire at the birds as fast as they can, trying to drop as many as they can. Then they grab what birds they can find. The birds they can't find in the dark, they leave behind.*

Carnage and waste are the rules in bird hunting, even during legal seasons and open hours. Thousands of wounded ducks and geese are not retrieved, left to rot in the marshes and fields. . . . *When I asked Wanda where hers had fallen, she wasn't sure.* Cripples, and there are many cripples made in this pastime, are still able to run and hide, eluding the hunter even if he's willing to spend time searching for them, which he usually isn't. . . . *It's one thing to run down a cripple in a picked bean field or a pasture, and quite another to watch a wing-tipped bird drop into a huge block of switch grass.* Oh nasty, nasty switch grass. A downed bird becomes invisible on the ground and is practically unfindable without a good dog, and few "waterfowlers" have them these days. They're hard to train—usually a professional has to do it—and most hunters can't be bothered. Birds are easy to tumble. . . . *Canada geese—blues and snows—can all take a good amount of shot. Brant are easily called and decoyed and come down easily. Ruffed grouse are hard to hit but easy to kill. Sharptails are harder to kill but easier to hit.* . . . It's just a nuisance to recover them. But it's fun, fun, fun swatting them down. . . . *There's distinct pleasure in watching a flock work to a good friend's gun.* . . .

Teal, the smallest of common ducks, are really easy to kill. Hunters in the South used to *practice* on teal in September, prior to the "serious" waterfowl season. But the birds were so diminutive and the limit so low (four a day) that many hunters felt it hardly worth going out and getting bit by mosquitoes to kill them. Enough did, however, brave the bugs and manage to "harvest" 165,000 of the little migrating birds in Louisiana in 1987 alone. *Shooting is usually best on opening day. By the second day you can sometimes detect a decline in local teal numbers. Areas may deteriorate to virtually no action by the third day.* . . . The area *deteriorates.* When a flock is wiped out, the skies are empty. *No action.*

Teal declined more sharply than any duck species except mallard last year; this baffles hunters. Hunters and their procurers—wildlife agencies—will *never* admit that hunting is responsible for the decimation of a species. John Turner, head of the Federal Fish and Wildlife Service, delivers the familiar and litanic line. Hunting is not the problem. *Pollution is the problem. Pesticides, urbanization, deforestation, hazardous waste,* and *wetlands destruction* is the problem. And drought! There's been a big drought! Antis should devote their energies to solving these problems if they care about wildlife, and leave the hunters alone. While the Fish and Wildlife Service is busily conducting experiments in cause and effect, like releasing mallard ducklings on a wetland sprayed with the insecticide ethyl parathion (they died—it was known they would, but you can never have enough studies that show guns aren't a duck's only problem), hunters are killing some two hundred million birds and animals each year. But these deaths are incidental to the problem, according to Turner. A factor, perhaps, but a *minor* one. Ducks Unlimited says the problem isn't hunting, it's *low recruitment* on the part of the birds. To the hunter, *birth* in the animal kingdom is *recruitment.* They wouldn't want to use an emotional, sentimental word like *birth.* The black duck, a very "popular" duck in the Northeast, so "popular," in fact, that game agencies felt that hunters couldn't be asked to refrain from shooting it, is scarce and getting scarcer. Nevertheless, it's still being hunted. *A number of studies are currently under way in an attempt to discover why black ducks are disappearing, Sports Afield* reports. Black ducks are disappearing because they've been shot out, their elimination being a dreadful example of game management, and managers who are loath to "displease" hunters. The skies—*flyways*—of America have been divided into four administrative regions, and the states, advised by a federal government coordinator, have to agree on policies.

There's always a lot of squabbling that goes on in flyway meetings—lots of complaints about short-stopping, for example. Short-stopping is the deliberate holding of birds in a state, often by feeding them in wildlife refuges, so that their southern migration is slowed or stopped. Hunters in the North get to kill more than hunters in the South. This isn't fair. Hunters demand equity in opportunities to kill.

Wildlife managers hate closing the season on anything. Closing the season on a species would indicate a certain amount of *mis*management and misjudgment at the very least—a certain reliance on overly optimistic winter counts, a certain overappeasement of hunters who would be "upset" if they couldn't kill their favorite thing. And worse, closing a season would be considered victory for the antis. Birdhunting "rules" are very complicated, but they all encourage killing. There are shortened seasons and split seasons and special seasons for "underutilized" birds. (Teal were very recently considered "underutilized.") The limit on coots is fifteen a day—shooting them, it's easy! They don't fly high—giving the hunter something to do while he waits in the blind. Some species are "protected," but bear in mind that hunters begin blasting away one half hour before sunrise and that most hunters can't identify a bird in the air even in broad daylight. Some of them can't identify birds in hand either, and even if they can (#%*! *I got me a canvasback, that duck's frigging protected* . . .), they are likely to bury unpopular or "trash" ducks so that they can continue to hunt the ones they "love."

Game "professionals," in thrall to hunters' "needs," will

not stop managing bird populations until they've doled out the final duck (*I didn't get my limit but I bagged the last one, by golly* . . .). The Fish and Wildlife Service services legal hunters as busily as any madam, but it is powerless in tempering the lusts of the illegal ones. Illegal kill is a monumental problem in the not-so-wonderful world of waterfowl. Excesses have always pervaded the "sport," and bird shooters have historically been the slobs and profligates of hunting. *Doing away with hunting would do away with a vital cultural and historical aspect of American life,* John Turner claims. So, do away with it. Do away with those who have already done away with so much. Do away with them before the birds they have pursued so relentlessly and for so long drop into extinction, sink, in the poet Wallace Stevens's words, "downward to darkness on extended wings."

"Quality" hunting is as rare as the Florida panther. What you've got is a bunch of guys driving over the plains, up the mountains, and through the woods with their stupid tag that cost them a couple of bucks and immense coolers full of beer and body parts. There's a price tag on the right to destroy living creatures for play, but it's not much. *A big-game hunting license is the greatest deal going since the Homestead Act,* Ted Kerasote writes in *Sports Afield*. *In many states residents can hunt big game for more than a month for about $20.* It's cheaper than taking the little woman out to lunch. It's cheap all right, and it's because killing animals is considered *recreation* and is underwritten by state and federal funds. In Florida, state moneys are routinely spent on "youth hunts," in which kids are guided to shoot deer from stands in wildlife-management areas. The organizers of these events say that these staged hunts *help youth to understand man's role in*

the ecosystem. (Drop a doe and take your place in the ecological community, son. . . .)

Hunters claim (they don't actually believe it but they've
learned to say it) that they're doing nonhunters a favor—for
if they didn't *use* wild animals, wild animals would be useless.
They believe that they're just *helping Mother Nature control
populations (you wouldn't want those deer to die of starvation,
would you?* . . .). They claim that their tiny fees provide *all*
Americans with wild lands and animals. (People who don't
hunt get to enjoy animals all year round while hunters get to
enjoy them only during hunting season. . . .) Ducks Unlimited feels that it, in particular, is a selfless provider and environmental champion. Although members spend most of
their money lobbying for hunters and raising ducks in pens
to release later over shooting fields, they do save some wetlands, mostly by persuading farmers not to fill them in. *See
that little pothole there the ducks like? Well, I'm gonna plant
more soybeans there if you don't pay me not to.* . . . Hunters
claim many nonsensical things, but the most nonsensical of
all is that they *pay their own way.* They do not pay their own
way. The *do* pay into a perverse wildlife-management system
that manipulates "stocks" and "herds" and "flocks" for hunters' killing pleasure, but these fees in no way cover the cost of
highly questionable ecological practices. For some spare
change . . . *the greatest deal going* . . . hunters can hunt
on public lands—national parks, state forests—preserves for
hunters!—which the nonhunting and antihunting public
pay for. (Access to private lands is becoming increasingly difficult for them, as experience has taught people that hunters
are obnoxious.) Hunters kill on millions of acres of land all
over America that is maintained with general taxpayer reve-

nue, but the most shocking, really twisted subsidization takes place on national wildlife refuges. Nowhere is the arrogance and the insidiousness of this small, aggressive minority more clearly demonstrated. Nowhere is the murder of animals, the manipulation of language, and the distortion of public intent more flagrant. The public perceives national wildlife refuges as safe havens, as sanctuaries for animals. And why wouldn't they? The word *refuge* of course *means* shelter from danger and distress. But the dweeby nonhunting public—they tend to be so literal. The word has been reinterpreted by management over time and now hunters are invited into more than half of the country's more than 440 wildlife "sanctuaries" each year to bang them up and kill more than half a million animals. This is called *wildlife-oriented recreation.* Hunters think of this as being no less than their due, claiming that refuge lands were purchased with duck stamps (. . . *our duck stamps paid for it . . . our duck stamps paid for it . . .*). Hunters equate those stupid stamps with the mystic, multiplying power of the Lord's loaves and fishes, but of ninety million acres in the Wildlife Refuge System, only three million were bought with hunting-stamp revenue. Most wildlife "restoration" programs in the states are translated into clearing land to increase deer habitats (so that too many deer will require hunting . . . you wouldn't want them to die of starvation, would you?) and trapping animals for restocking and study (so hunters can shoot more of them). Fish and game agencies hustle hunting—instead of conserving wildlife, they're killing it. It's time for them to get in the business of protecting and preserving wildlife and creating balanced ecological systems instead of pimping for hunters who want their deer/duck/pheasant/ turkey—animals stocked to be shot.

Hunters' self-serving arguments and lies are becoming more preposterous as non-hunters awake from their long, albeit troubled, sleep. Sport hunting is immoral; it should be made illegal. Hunters are persecutors of nature who should be prosecuted. They wield a disruptive power out of all proportion to their numbers, and pandering to their interests—the special interests of a group that just wants to kill things—is mad. It's preposterous that every year less than 7 percent of the population turns the skies into shooting galleries and the woods and fields into abattoirs. It's time to stop actively supporting and passively allowing hunting, and time to stigmatize it. It's time to stop being conned and cowed by hunters, time to stop pampering and coddling them, time to get them off the government's duck-and-deer dole, time to stop thinking of wild animals as "resources" and "game," and start thinking of them as sentient beings that deserve our wonder and respect, time to stop allowing hunting to be creditable by calling it "sport" and "re-creation." Hunters make wildlife *dead, dead, dead*. It's time to wake up to this indisputable fact. As for the hunters, it's long past check-out time.

RUDOLPH WURLITZER

My First Pet

IN THE SUMMER of 1969, I was a confirmed minimalist, not to mention nihilist. My only literary effort that summer was to make a list of the first twenty-one objects in my newly acquired rent-controlled apartment on East Twenty-third Street and publish the list in a small obscure review. But even that effort seemed more than I could handle.

For months, the list, which included a knife and fork, bed sheets, coffee cup and pencil, remained frozen, as did the rest of my life. I had broken up with my girlfriend. My first novel, a solipsistic journey into the fallibility of my own mind, or what I took to be my own mind, had not yet come out. I had a few deranged friends who seemed as paralyzed and numb as I obviously was. We all seemed to be barely moving within the inverted heat wave that hung over the city for months like a blanket from hell, choking us with its smog and steaming dog shit. I had no job and no prospects. I smoked dope from morning to night, despite the government's new Operation Intercept program, which consisted of spraying all the grass with paraquat, thus helping speed to be introduced to the inner cities. I ate all my meals at the Greek coffee shop on the corner and I tried, unsuccessfully, to control the flow of information about a world that seemed to have gone berserk. Every day a steady stream of body bags was flown back from Vietnam. Bobby Kennedy and Martin Luther King had already been murdered the year before but this summer had its own unique signature. It was the season of the Manson murders, Brian Jones's o.d., and Woodstock, the party of parties which, in retrospect, seemed to announce the end of the decade as well as all parties forever. I lived as if my shoe was nailed to the floor of a huge waiting room and yet I didn't know what I was waiting for. Only that whatever was coming down the road would not be savory.

The twenty-second object in my apartment was a secondhand television set, which I placed in the middle of my bare living room floor. I bought the TV on Friday, July 18th, the same day that Ted Kennedy's car went off the bridge in Chappaquiddick, causing the death of Mary Jo Kopechne. But I wasn't aware of this at the time. My only motivation toward being "hooked up" was to follow the Mets and be a witness to the first moon landing, set for that Sunday night.

With that historic event in mind, I copped a few tabs of acid and invited two friends to join me. One was an out-of-work filmmaker on a solipsistic journey of his own, the other was his girlfriend, a young English beauty with a wide sensual mouth and a curtain of hip-length hair, who I was secretly in love with.

Only a few flashes, like faraway heat lightning, remain from that night: Neil Armstrong setting foot on the surface of the moon. Hysterical laughter followed by an awkward attempt toward a "three-way" ménage that left the English girl pouting and weeping in the corner, her boyfriend in a sullen rage and myself lying in the dark in the bathtub for four hours watching a parade of visualizations that ranged from galactic naval battles to cosmic dissections of waterbugs and cockroaches.

The next morning, as I stumbled through the wretched emptiness of my apartment, I came upon a message painted crudely on the kitchen wall with huge yellow strokes: BETTER AN OLD DEMON THAN A NEW GOD.

Clearly, it was time for a change.

Blinded by the fury of my own alienation, I stumbled into the street. In front of me was a pet store. I found myself in a world of birds, dogs, cats, snakes and fish. A world that smelled of shit and animal feed; all the frenzied animal, serpent, and fish activity muted by the sound of gurgling water pouring into dozens of aquariums.

In this entire display of potential love and devotion, only one object was capable of holding my attention. Along the far wall, submerged in a low tank, lurked a motionless creature with a crusted barnacled back, its ridge shaped like an ancient prehistoric fossil. The creature was undefinable and mysterious, even ominous in its stillness. No moist-eyed pleadings or barks of welcome. No promises. No sympathy or affirmation. This creature was beyond charm, beyond friendship, beyond communication. It was the right ticket. Impeccable. Immovable. Possibly even immortal. "A Mata Mata turtle," the pet store owner said with imperious solemnity. "Probably four or five hundred years old."

I bought it. Tank and all.

After I had installed the tank on the kitchen table and deposited the creature within, I looked up Mata Mata in my Webster dictionary, the sixteenth object in my apartment. The description of Nog, named after the title of my novel, was mercifully brief: "A pleurodiran turtle (*Chelys fimbriata*) of the rivers of Guiana and northern Brazil. It reaches a length of three feet, and is remarkable for its rough shell, long neck, and fleshy fimbriae on its head and neck."

Once a week I deposited a goldfish into Nog's tank. The fish would swim, unsuspecting, around the tank, sometimes for days, until suddenly Nog's neck would extend like a furious erection, slashing out of its shell, the slit of a mouth opening and the goldfish disappearing. All in less than a blink. No motion wasted. No evidence of satisfaction or lust. After the great gulp, the eyes would close and the reptilian neck would shrink into the body, not to move again until the next feeding.

Through that summer my relationship to Nog was steady and ritualistic. The feedings marked the passage of time. Weeks passed. Fall came and then winter. Over a dozen goldfish had been consumed. Then sixteen. Then twenty. The objects in my apartment increased, until now there were over fifty. My brain was getting crowded as well. Another girlfriend came and went, another book was begun and discarded. The only solid dependable being in my frayed mandala was Nog. And yet I began to think too much about the goldfish. I found myself sitting before the tank for hours, waiting for Nog's neck to emerge from his shell. Once I put two goldfish in the tank, then three. Nog reacted by not eating for two weeks and then one morning, staggering back from the bathroom, I noticed all three goldfish were gone. I worried about indigestion. But what vet could I go to? I became obsessed with the possibility of Nog dying, about having to flush him down the toilet and thus ending a life that had existed for over four or five centuries.

And then I began to feel guilty about the goldfish. Despite my resolve not to interfere with this ancient cannibalistic ritual, I even became attached to a few of them. I felt like a monster, keeping them alive in a separate tank just to drop them into Nog's arena. When the great trial comes for all sentient beings at the end of time, I knew I would be condemned to be fed to a primeval beast or minotaur, my remains to be oozed out of its asshole into the great muck and slime of the "gods' aquarium."

Finally, I could bear my life in New York no longer. Too many objects. Too many goldfish. Too many thoughts. After subletting my apartment to a girlfriend of a girlfriend with explicit instructions about Nog's maintenance, I drove west, pointing my hubcaps toward the setting sun.

Six months later, I drifted back. The girlfriend of the girlfriend was gone and so was Nog. The ex-boyfriend of the girlfriend was in her place.

The ex-boyfriend explained that his ex-girlfriend had freaked out about Nog and did, in fact, try to flush him down the toilet. Only a fist fight saved Nog's life. They finally agreed to give Nog to the ex-girlfriend's sister who, in turn, passed Nog on to a saxophone player who lent him to a roadie on the upper West Side. Where he still was.

But I was only passing through New York and never made an attempt to retrieve Nog. For all I know he's still up on the West Side, eating goldfish once a week. Or perhaps he's been thrown into the Hudson River or is back in a pet store waiting to be sold. Three or four hundred years from now, long after the upper West Side and this entire wretched civilization has disappeared, it comforts me to think that Nog might still be alive, waiting for a goldfish to swim by.

Notes on the Contributors

William S. Burroughs is the author of *Junkie, Naked Lunch, The Place of Dead Roads, Cities of the Red Night, Queer*, and many other works. He is a member of the American Academy of Arts and Letters, and a Commandeur de l'Ordre des Arts et Lettres of France. He lives in Lawrence, Kansas.

Lars Eighner is the author of *Travels with Lizbeth*, a memoir, and several books of short stories. A member of the Texas Institute of Letters and a recipient of the Pushcart Prize, he lives in Austin, Texas.

Richard Ford lives in New Orleans and in northern Montana.

Janet Hamill is the author of *Troublante, The Temple*, and *Nostalgia of the Infinite*. Her poetry and fiction have appeared in anthologies such as *Up Late: American Poetry Since 1970, The Low-Tech Manual*, and *The Unmade Bed*. Some of the numerous magazines and journals that have published her work are *Bomb, City Lights Review, Colorado North Review, Kansas Quarterly, Exquisite Corpse, Poetry Flash*, and the *Hart Crane Newsletter*. Following sojourns in Mexico,

Europe, and Africa, and a twenty-year residence in Manhattan, she now resides in upstate New York.

Barbara Kruger is an artist whose work has appeared throughout America, Europe, and Japan in galleries, newspapers, magazines, and museums, and on billboards, matchbooks, TV programs, T-shirts, postcards, and shopping bags.

Fran Lebowitz is the author of *Metropolitan Life* and *Social Studies*. She is currently writing a novel called *Exterior Signs of Wealth*.

Heather Lewis is the author of *House Rules* (Talese/Doubleday, 1994), which received the New Voice Award from the Writer's Voice Project. She was born in Mount Kisco, New York, in 1961 and now lives in New York City, where she has worked as a bookseller, an editor, and a freelance copy editor.

The story "Mouse," first published in *Audubon* magazine in 1964, was **Faith McNulty**'s debut as a wildlife reporter. Since then she has written many other pieces about her meetings with wildlife, most of them published in *The New Yorker* magazine and in book form in *The Wildlife Stories of Faith McNulty* (Doubleday, 1980). She has also written a number of books for children, many of them about animals.

Taylor Mead is an Obie award-winning actor, a filmmaker, and the author of three books, including the forthcoming *Son of Andy Warhol*. He lives in New York City.

Leonard Michaels's most recent books are *Sylvia,* an autobiographical memoir, and *To Feel These Things,* a collection of essays, both published by Mercury House.

Duane Michals is a photographer who also writes, and was last seen around Gramercy Park.

Dean Ripa's list of field captures of venomous snakes reads like a Who's Who of the most dangerous on earth. They include King Cobras, Black Forest Cobras, Spitting Cobras, Green Mambas, Kraits, Gaboon vipers, Rhinoceros vipers, Puff Adders, and many more serpentine rarities. He was the first person in the world to breed the Central American Bushmaster in captivity. He has traveled extensively in over fifty countries on five continents, and lived in many of them as well. He has been bitten five times by venomous snakes. He has no amputations.

Ann Rower's story collection, *If You're a Girl,* was published by Native Agents (Semiotext[e]). Her second is in progress and is called *Armed Response.* She has collaborated with the Wooster Group (*The Babysitter in LSD, Situations of Confrontation*), Chris Kraus, and Vito Ricci. She is completing a biography of her uncle, lyricist Leo Robin ("Thanks for the Memory," "Diamonds Are a Girl's Best Friend"). Her most recent accomplishment is prying herself, after twenty years, out of the mean streets of Downtown (New York), no mean feat.

Barbet Schroeder's films include *More, Maitresse, Koko, A Talking Gorilla, Idi Amin Dada, Barfly, Reversal of Fortune,* and *Single White Female.*

Hunt Slonem is a painter who has lived and worked with some seventy birds at his studio at Houston and Bowery in New York for the past twenty years. He has had 120 one-person shows internationally.

Patti Smith's recent books include *Woolgathering* (Hanuman Books) and *Early Work, 1970–1979* (Norton).

Susan Swan is a novelist and a professor of humanities at York University in Toronto. Her fiction has been published in Canada, the United States, Germany, and Britain. Her most recent novel, *The Wives of Bath* (Knopf, 1993), a gothic tale about a girl's boarding school, was short-listed for the Guardian fiction prize in England.

Emma Tennant has written many novels, of which the latest, *Pemberly,* is a sequel to *Pride and Prejudice.* She lives in London.

Lynne Tillman is the author of *Haunted Houses, Absence Makes the Heart, Motion Sickness,* and, most recently, *Cast in Doubt* and *The Madame Realism Complex.* Her essays and fiction appear regularly in *Art in America, Bomb,* and the *Village Voice Literary Supplement.* She is the co-director and writer of the independent feature film *Committed.*

"The Bears at Central Park" are among many four-footed denizens of the big city to figure in **Guy Trebay**'s collected tales of New York, *In the Place to Be*. A staff writer at the *Village Voice*, Trebay also contributes to *The New Yorker* and other national magazines.

William Wegman is an artist well known for his painting and drawings, and even more well known for his photographs of his dogs, Man Ray, Fay Ray, and, more recently, Battina.

Joy Williams is a novelist and short story writer. In 1993 she received the Strauss Living Award from the American Academy of Arts and Letters. She lives in Florida and Arizona.

Rudolph Wurlitzer has written four novels, *Nog, Quake, Flats,* and *Slow Fade,* as well as a travel book, *Hard Travel to Sacred Places*. He has also written numerous screenplays.

Acknowledgments

About the Editor

Gary Indiana is a contributing editor of *Interview*, an editor-at-large for *Bomb*, and a staff writer for the *Village Voice*. His books include *Scar Tissue*, *Horse Crazy*, and *Gone Tomorrow*. He lives in New York City.